A Barter To Providence

How the World Really Works

W. D. Moore

A Bartender's Guide to Providence:
How the World Really Works

Copyright © 2010 by William D. Moore. All rights reserved.

All Scripture quotations are taken from the New King James Version.

ISBN 978-0-9842704-0-8

16

15 14 13 12 11 10

7 6 5 4 3 2 1

Printed in China

Published by: Your Life As History, Inc.

Ezra Ministries, Inc., Loami, Illinois
Mailing Address:
P.O. Box 428
Winnetka, IL 60093
217-652-3525; William Moore, a Director

References: Sovereignty – Chastening – Providence - Christianity

The girl of my dreams is the girl in my arms. My Lois still causes me to catch my breath a bit when I first see her in the morning. She is, for me, like no other. Her drive permits me the time to write, and no one I've met is so generous with encouragement. Lois, thank you.

Eileen Moore, my friend, has inspired me to finish writing this little book. I talk about being courageous, Eileen is. Nobility and grace are wed in her. I hope this makes her blush. A hundred years from now she and I will be marveling at God's providence in her life. The suffering? We'll both understand it. The pain? We'll both be thankful for it. Eileen's husband, Charles, is my friend. Providence brought him, and I intend to cherish him until Providence takes him away.

A special thank-you to my new friend, Sue Taylor, who diligently and patiently edited this effort for me. Her changes and suggestions made the whole process sweeter.

Contents

Preface	6
Introduction	10
Chapter 1: Good News Depends On Your Perspective	17
Chapter 2: The Foundation: Our Texts	25
Chapter 3: Plain Talk	44
Chapter 4: A Primer on Providence	59
Chapter 5: Jumping into the Deep End: Concurrence and Humanity's Freedom	76
Chapter 6: Providential Chastening	99
Chapter 7: Bill, I Still Want to Avoid Chastenings	121
Chapter 8: A Few Questions about 1 Kings 22: 34	139
Chapter 9: I Had a Rough Childhood—*So What?*	158
Chapter 10: Beauty Bests the Beast	177
Chapter 11: A Command As Rigorous As It Was Cruel	204
Chapter 12: I Can't See What God's Doing—Isn't That Important?	225
Conclusion	244

Preface

When good things happen in your life, do you thank God? When bad things happen in your life, do you thank God? There is no typo in the previous sentence. Does it seem ridiculous to ask if you thank God when bad things happen to you? Is it equally ridiculous to ask if you thank God when good things happen?

Allow me to probe a bit deeper. How do you and I "know" when something that happens to us is "good"? Likewise, are "bad things" so universally agreed upon that you and I would never have a differing opinion about any event being "good" or "bad"?

How do I decide if the promotion I receive at work is good? Can a promotion be bad? Of course, it can. Suppose I am promoted to the position of principal because of my excellence as a teacher. Could that promotion, which brings more money into my household and brings me greater esteem from colleagues, ruin my life? What if the skills that make me an excellent teacher are not the same ones that would make me an excellent principal? What if I lack the required administrative skills? What if the promotion makes me prideful? What if the promotion takes a contented duck from his pond and plops him into the ocean? Is that a "good thing"?

Consider your nineteen-year-old son who is in love with the beautiful prom queen. He is smitten with her and so distracted that his grades slip and he has no time for his old friends. Early one morning the phone rings, and amid the tears and wailing you decipher that last night he discovered the prom queen drunk in the backseat of a red MINI Cooper with the dean of the art school. Is this bad news to you? No. It's good news. Your son has likely avoided a relationship that could have ruined his life.

What about your son? His sobs testify to his view—it's the worst thing that could have happened to him. Is he right? Yes and no. Pain, especially heart pain, is a bad thing. On the other hand, eventually—perhaps on his wedding day—he will conclude that what happened was a good thing. He values his old friends again, he reapplies himself to his studies, and his distrust of girls keeps him safe until he meets that "one in a thousand" who becomes his bride.

Good things and bad things require more than a cursory discussion. In fact, "all things," as a category, warrant an investigation *if* we want to understand *our lives.*

The quest to understand our lives and the search for meaning in our lives is as old as humanity. Most people I speak with believe they have a firm grasp on the meaning of life in general and on the meaning of their lives in particular. That seems odd to me because they never seem to have a clear perspective on "good things" and "bad things," which is foundational to any accurate understanding of life.

Let me raise a question I hinted at earlier: Where does God fit into this? We do thank Him, right—at least for what we perceive to be good? Why do we thank Him or, for that matter, blame Him for "things" that happen? To answer that question, we first need to ask another:

Does God Actually Govern This World?

Does He influence people and events, initiate actions, intervene in our affairs, and allow particular developments to take place? Consider carefully this passage from the book of Romans:

> All things work together for good to those who love God, to those who are the called according to His purpose.
> (Romans 8:28)

All things work together for good. For whom—believers? What about unbelievers? What does "God's purpose" mean? Now you know why I've written this little book. I need to understand my life and the meaning of it. I must grasp my history before I can grasp my future. For that matter, shouldn't I understand my own history before I try to pontificate about the history of humankind?

Perhaps what we need is a plain vanilla discussion of good things, bad things, and random arrows.

If the man doesn't believe as we do, we say he is a crank, and that settles it. I mean, it does nowadays, because we can't burn him.
—Mark Twain

Introduction

This book is arranged in a question-and-answer style which I hope will facilitate small-group Bible studies as well as bartender/customer discourses. In my experience, Bible studies and tavern talks that raise questions encourage additional questions and engage people's minds.

The question-and-answer style is also an accommodation to the changed character of both Bible study groups and their counterparts in the world, barroom buddies. Both groups, it seems, are unwilling to read more than a few pages at a sitting:

> The fact is, people don't read anymore.
> —Steve Jobs

Mr. Jobs' pragmatic comment reflects the predictable end of a trend noted more than one hundred fifty years ago by one great reader:

> Most people have learned to read to serve a paltry convenience, as they have learned to cipher in order to keep accounts and not be cheated in trade; but of reading as a noble, intellectual exercise they know little or nothing.
> —Henry David Thoreau

In this little book I will attempt to establish the fact that the "real" way the "real" world works is the way the Bible teaches. The Bible reveals that God governs the natural world as well as the lives of all of his creatures. No detail escapes His government. God guides, oversees, and directs both His creation and His creatures. This simple, straightforward statement will suffice for now. We'll get to a more comprehensive definition later. It is my hope the "Bartender's Guide" format will promote discussions about the way the "real" world works.

If the paths through the woods of providence seem always to be crisscrossing each other, it's because they do. But as your guide, I ask you to bear with me. I *will* get you through the woods eventually. Because old paths are the most tried paths, I will ask you to retrace your steps several times. I tend to be a slow learner, and I'll assume the same is true of you. A sprint through the woods seldom leaves a lasting impression. A leisurely stroll up and down and back and forth on the paths is best. At that pace, we can smell the woods, taste the air, and listen for peculiar sounds. I promise you an adventure, as well as a safe passage.

First, though, I am always attempting to understand life in light of what the Scriptures teach. Our mission at Ezra Ministries, of which I'm a director, is to study the Scriptures in order to apply them to our lives. Second, we wish to help others apply those truths to their lives and thus make disciples:

> Ezra had prepared his heart to seek the Law of the LORD, and to do it, and to teach statutes and ordinances in Israel.
> (Ezra 7:10)

My friends will testify that I am fond of seeing life as a gauntlet to be run. I imagine the years of my life arranged in two parallel lines, leaving only a narrow gap that I must run through while the years batter me on my way home to heaven. Job had a similar philosophy:

> Man who is born of woman
> Is of few days and full of trouble.
> (Job 14:1)

I believe all of us—at least all believers—are buffeted from the crib to the grave. All of this happens not only under God's watchful eye but also under His powerful hand. We believers are sheep being shepherded by the great Shepherd. Plainness and clarity are always my goals, and if I fall short, please judge me kindly, as I'm truly just an itinerant Bible teacher without formal training. So, be charitable if you will. My aim is God's glory and the exaltation of His name.

A special thank-you goes to Thomas Watson, who published a wonderful little book titled *A Divine Cordial* in 1663. Watson suffered affliction for his faithfulness to Christ and drew his strength from the Scriptures. God has made Watson's insights a source of blessing to me. In 1986, the Banner of Truth Trust republished Watson's book under the title *All Things for Good*. I recommend it under either title, although the Puritan style can be a little strange to modern ears.

I would also like to thank Dr. R. C. Sproul for his many books and teachings on providence and God's sovereignty. Third, I'm grateful to Dr. John Gerstner, now in heaven several years, who once responded to me by fax, "Mr. Moore, do you ever think before you write?" When I see him, I will ask whether his note was penned as affectionately as I think it was. I *have* learned to think before I write, and I hope the finished product is helpful to you as you run your own gauntlet.

Finally, a special note of thanks goes to Marie, still the best bartender I've ever met. Little Ricky's is blessed to have you. Tell Patrick I said so, will you? Marie, conversations with you were instrumental in the writing of this little book.

Author's Note

As a youth I learned to gamble, and I loved it passionately. For ten years I made my living by shooting pool, playing cards, rolling dice, and working a variety of illegal scams. Scuffling, hustling, and deception were not only my pursuits, they were also my passions. Bookmaking, that is, taking bets on sporting events, appeared to be my destiny. After all, I had the necessary "gifts"—a vicious  temper, a certain recklessness toward life, and an utter disregard for others. Woven in among my other pursuits were burglaries, thefts, and assaults. Those were busy times. I followed Mark Twain's advice and didn't let "my schooling get in the way of my education." Unfortunately, I required very little sleep, three hours per night at most. This left a great deal of time for sinning. I attempt to speak lightheartedly of those days, but when I'm alone and quiet, shame often washes over me like a chilly wave.

Women became human beings to me when I turned thirty— okay, maybe forty is more accurate. I'm sad to say that this was more than ten years after my conversion to Christianity. Sanctification is a process. But I'm grateful that our gracious God has changed me. Most "normal" emotions are now within my grasp.

Why have I told you this? Because my wife told me to, and Ashley, my young friend, agreed it was best. They believe that who I am is important to what I say. You'll be the judge of the validity of their sentiment. An understanding of the author does permit the reader to better appreciate anecdotal information and examples as they are sprinkled throughout the book.

Several years ago I considered writing a sort of autobiography. I titled it *Dork in the Dark.* Some of the stories were interesting and funny, but I wasn't certain the pathetic exploits of a small-time, small-town moron would be of interest to anyone other than behavioral therapists and literate felons. These are two groups that could easily switch positions in life and be content, I might add. In fact, it would be a considerable vocational upgrade for the behavioral therapists. My old friend, Bill McKenzie, reminded me that I should remind you, my reader, that this little dig at behavioral therapists was not intended to include all behavioral therapists. Bill and his lovely bride are excluded. After all, Bill offered helpful suggestions in the writing of this book! My writing fever broke, however, and I abandoned the project.

Some time ago my beloved Lois suggested I try writing again. Wiser now than a young man could ever be, I obeyed. The autobiography morphed into *A Strange Thing Happened on My Way to Hell,* an effort to praise God for His grace in regenerating an atheistic numbskull. *Wallowing in the World: A Peek at Earthly-Mindedness* followed. That title is my attempt to change me from an earthly-minded man to a heavenly-minded one. The book you're reading now is number three. If my pilgrimage is prolonged, I intend for my fourth effort to be *Naked Folks Have Very Little Effect on Society.* The title is a paraphrase of an old Twain quote. The book will be a primer, I hope, on how to witness to the world and in the world. I'm persuaded that Christian decisionalism has spawned a generation of Christian folks who couldn't hold a decent discussion in a tavern about life and Christ if the church's life depended on it. Come to think of it, it does. This book will raise the usual objections to Christianity and complaints about Christianity and, I hope, handle them. Last, I've set my heart on writing *A Hypocrite's Handbook,* which will most assuredly be autobiographical.

Now you know—or at least you think you do—who is challenging you. You ought to question every point I make. Search the Scriptures to see if what I say is true. I've already warned you that I'm not formally educated, and I've readily confessed to you that character has always been an issue where I'm concerned. So, proceed at your own risk.

I was a chain gang of fools under one head of hair.
—W. D. Moore

1

Good News Depends on Your Perspective

That "good things" work for our good is generally an agreeable notion to most people. But how "bad things" can be good and work for good requires some serious discussion and is certain to engender some disagreement. More precisely, we all want to know how *bad* things that happen to *us* can be good for *us*. Allow me to begin to respond to that question by introducing Sascha.

One sultry night some two years ago, a lone, pretty, blonde girl paced nervously back and forth, as unable to stand still as the freight train blocking the crossing was unwilling to budge. The harsh clanging of the warning signal that punctured the night seemed to quicken its pace in an effort to mirror the solitary figure's increasingly agitated motions. Midnight was history, and Sascha had a 9:00 a.m. court appearance that would determine whether she would be allowed to retain custody of her children, Cecilia and Judge. The possibility of losing her three- and five-year-olds heightened Sascha's frustration. Emboldened by the alcohol she had promised the court she would abstain from, Sascha mounted the coupling between the train cars, much as she had done many times before.

The train lurched forward. Sascha tumbled, and the clanging of the railroad signal was drowned in a scream. Only the stars can corroborate what happened next. Sascha rolled away from the wheels in time to save her life—but not her leg. The train glided into the darkness, unaware of the prominent part it was playing in the drama that is Sascha's life. For fifteen minutes tears rushed down Sascha's cheeks as she elevated her nearly severed leg toward the moon in an effort to slow the loss of blood.

I said above that only the stars witnessed the sad event, but that's untrue. The sovereign Lord who hung those stars so long ago and still assures they don't fall today was watching with a Father's eye. Someone heard Sascha's plaintive cries and extended pity. She was rushed to the hospital, where, the next day, her leg was amputated. Later that day, she spoke with me—her dad—on the phone.

Even now tears fill my eyes when I think of what must have been the sights and sounds of that terrible night. A daughter's fear, sadness, and anguish weigh heavily on a father's heart. That this event qualifies as a "bad thing" seems uncontestable. With Sascha's career as a waitress clearly over and the court certain now to decide that she was an unfit mother, Sascha's life was tragic, to put the best spin on it.

Reaching for my glasses as I reached for the phone, I saw from the alarm that it was 3:00 in the morning. The fact that I was vacationing in Greece meant that there was a seven-hour difference between where I was and home in Illinois. In my sleepy fog, I couldn't remember whether to add seven hours or subtract them, but the feeling in my stomach steeled me for the news. Sascha's brother, Ebben, was on the phone explaining to me what had happened and how he was being "Dad" to his sister in my absence.

Sascha's voice was strong when she got on the phone, and only slightly quickened. She hated bothering me; she hated ruining my vacation; and there was no need in her mind for me to rush home, she said. Oh, and by the way, those Bible studies on the book of Judges were on her mind: "God brought affliction to His Israelites from love, right? They had sinned and wouldn't repent, right? God, in mercy, had opened their ears by suffering, right? I am just like them, right, Dad? I have to go—love you, Dad."

Sascha didn't lose her children, now sports a fine new leg, and is struggling, as we all do, to master the computer. The best thing that ever happened to her? You guessed it! According to Sascha, it was losing her leg. Her prosthesis is an abiding reminder of God's love and grace. She lost her leg but regained her senses. Her body suffered, but her soul prospered. Sascha viewed her life as another chapter in the book of Judges. Her father marvels at her wisdom and understanding.

After reading a draft of this little book, Sascha phoned me.

"Dad, there's one thing I didn't tell you in the story."

"What?"

"I only began crying when the dogs started barking. I heard them, and it sounded like they were getting nearer. I thought I was Jezebel and that God was sending the dogs to eat me. I broke down." Apparently Sascha had also attended a Bible study on 2 Kings.

When we were covering Jezebel's demise in our Bible study group, I thought Sascha had dozed off. Apparently I was mistaken. The Word of God was imbedded in her mind. God sent the dogs to fetch it from Sascha's memory bank and used the story of Jezebel to bring about Sascha's change of heart.

Is Sascha's experience evidence that "bad things" (afflictions) can work for good? The loss of her leg was devastating for Sascha, a terrible trauma for her *body*. But her *soul* has prospered because of the loss. Certainly the interests of one's soul are superior to the welfare of one's body, right? Let's be clear: Bad things in and of themselves *are* bad things. By definition, bad things are never good things. Just in case you missed what I'm saying, permit me to be more plain: When an unbeliever loses her leg, it is a bad thing. When a believer loses her leg, it is a bad thing as well. The difference lies with God. God sovereignly transforms bad things, or afflictions, into good things in the lives of believers. Bad things sanctified by God become servants of good for God's children.

For clarity, I must add that for unbelievers, suffering is tragic. In fact, let me go one step further. Dr. John Gerstner was on point when he used to say, "Anything, good or bad, that happens to an unbeliever is a tragedy." Read that again slowly. Can perfect health and limitless riches be tragic? Yes, yes, and — emphatically — *yes!*

> There was a certain rich man who was clothed in purple and fine linen and fared sumptuously every day. But there was a certain beggar named Lazarus, full of sores, who was laid at his gate, desiring to be fed with the crumbs which fell from the rich man's table. Moreover the dogs came and licked his sores. So it was that the beggar died, and was carried by the angels to Abraham's bosom. The rich man also died and was buried. And being in torments in Hades, he

> lifted up his eyes and saw Abraham afar off, and Lazarus in his bosom. . . . [Being tormented in flames, the rich man implored Abraham to send Lazarus with water for his tongue.] But Abraham said, "Son, remember that in your lifetime you received your good things, and likewise Lazarus evil things; but now he is comforted and you are tormented."
> (Luke 16:19-25)

Was Jesus teaching that it's a sin to be rich and live well? I don't think so. We aren't told that the rich man achieved success through theft, deception, or fraud. We *can* conclude, however, that living among and for plenty and pleasure is dangerous. To many it proves spiritually fatal. Riches tempt their holders to luxury, ingratitude, and forgetfulness about their soul's interests. As Dr. Gerstner noted, all things that happen to an unbeliever, including receiving "good things" in this lifetime, often prove to be both tragic and lethal. Transitory happiness may consist in ease and luxury. But true happiness (that is, joy) consists in profit and comfort for the soul outside of temporal circumstances, for the soul is the person.

> Happiness lies not in those things a man may enjoy and still be miserable forever.

—Thomas Brooks

This supposes that I understand, as Sascha did and the rich man found out, that I am two parts, a body and a soul. Remember, our text states that "all things work together for good to those who love God." It is true and can be true only if God overrules the events of my life so that they are made to work for my *soul's* good. The beggar, Lazarus, suffered "bad things" in this temporary world, but his "good things" came in the next, the eternal world. In light of that, does his life seem tragic?

> I've never quite gotten over the wonder of it all.
> —Gypsy Smith

Understanding my past, present, and future is important to me, and I'm sure it's the same for you. This book is my attempt to help us attain a biblical perspective on life, knowing that a biblical view is an infallible view.
Therefore, I've chosen three key passages of Scripture as the foundation for our discussion. Those passages are as follows:

> **Romans 8:28:** We know that all things work together for good to those who love God, to those who are the called according to His purpose.
>
> **Hebrews 12:5-8:** You have forgotten the exhortation which speaks to you as sons: "My son, do not despise the chastening of the Lord, nor be discouraged when you are rebuked by Him; For whom the Lord loves, He chastens, and scourges every son whom He receives." If you endure chastening, God deals with you as sons; for what son is there whom a father does not chasten? But if you are without chastening, of which all have become partakers, then you are illegitimate and not sons.
>
> **1 Kings 22:34:** A certain man drew a bow at random and struck the King of Israel between the joints of his armor. So he said to the driver of the chariot, "Turn

around and take me out of the battle, for I am wounded."

I hope our discussion will shine a light on our lives and perhaps cause us first to reevaluate our pasts. If our view of the past is altered, our view of the present and future must necessarily change.

Christians in this age are seeking significance in all the wrong places, namely in worldly pursuits. Silly creatures we are! We have eternal significance. God Himself is governing, directing, and sustaining our lives, and not for some meager earthly glory but for His eternal glory. Perhaps I can help us to see this.

We shall delve into the idea of "chastening," and we shall annihilate any notions we may have of *chance* and *fate*. These two words describe something that doesn't exist. They are descriptive only of an unbeliever's delusions.

Now that I've whetted your appetite, let's proceed to a consideration of our texts.

We are prisoners now and pupils in a school where often our best rewards appear to us to be our punishments.
—E. A. Robinson

2

The Foundation: Our Texts

At the end of chapter 1, I introduced the three Scripture texts that form the basis for our discussion in this book. Now we need to take a closer look at each of them to see where they lead us in our quest to understand the idea of God's providence.

Romans 8:28

> We know that all things work together for good to those who love God, to those who are the called according to His purpose.

Earlier in Romans 8, the apostle Paul speaks of sufferings. Now in this great verse he concludes that even our sufferings in this life are instruments used by God to promote our salvation.

The point we must focus on is that *what is good for believers is that which does good for their souls*. Reread that sentence, will you? Do God's merciful providences work good for my soul? Yes. They are part of the "all things" of Romans 8:28. Do God's afflicting providences work good for my soul? Yes. They, too, are part of "all things." This verse, I believe, is chiefly addressing the question of a believer's afflictions. It is not a strange thing for a disciple of Christ to be surrounded by troubles in this world. What is compelling is the fact that for true Christians, these troubles work for the good of their souls.

The great Physician makes smiling providences and frowning providences work together, as multiple medications might in the case of a cancer patient. One medicine attacks the cancer cells while another strengthens the patient. Each cancer patient receives a different drug cocktail because each patient has a different temperament, physique, and cancer. In the same way, God perfectly designs a "cocktail" of afflictions and blessings for each of His children.

The key is that God cannot err in concocting the potion a "patient" needs. God also has ample power to assure that "all things" in the potion of afflictions and blessings work together for the patient's good. Remember, it's the soul's interest we are speaking of. Am I comparing a believer's life to a chemotherapy treatment? Absolutely.

God governs all adversities so that what we commonly think of as "bad things" are made to work for our soul's best interests. Can "bad things"/afflictions be made to benefit us temporally also? Certainly. In the book of Genesis, Joseph's enslavement and later imprisonment led to his ability to provide for his family during a time of famine. We'll look more closely at that in chapter 12.

Likewise, God still makes afflictions work for temporal good today. A friend phoned a few years ago to tell me his associate in his law practice had been murdered the previous evening. My friend, let's call him Ted, outlined the grisly details for me and ended by revealing that he was the primary suspect. The local newspaper drowned my friend in speculation and innuendo so completely that he was forced to leave town—which only fueled further speculation that he was guilty of the atrocity. With his law practice and reputation gone, Ted had little choice but to move nearer home and open a small office that handled personal-injury cases.

Was what happened terrible? Was it unfair? Yes, it was terrible and unfair. But God was governing all of it for Ted's good.

Months later Ted phoned to say the real murderer had been apprehended. By the way, he said, "shortly after I opened my little office, a gentleman came in who was poor and needed my help because he had been injured on the job and then unjustly fired by his boss. We've just received a substantial settlement offer that will solve my client's financial problems as well as my own. If I hadn't been unfairly persecuted, I wouldn't have been in my little office to meet and help this poor man."

Make no mistake, God is still ordering "all things" for the good of His followers.

Yet in Romans 8:28, Paul is emphasizing not the temporal good but the eternal good. And he is further stressing that God governs "bad things" so that they work for good *only for believers*. This promise is not for unbelievers. The persons this passage is talking about are "those who love God . . . the called according to His purpose."

There is certainty to it. "We know," the verse begins. There is no wavering about it, no room for doubt. *We know*.

"All things work together for good." Do you see room for any exceptions in the word *all*? Does it say that all things sometimes or occasionally work together for good? If not, then we believers ought not kill ourselves with cares and anxieties. All of God's various dealings with us *will* work for our good.

"The called according to His purpose" refers to all true believers while at the same time beautifully reminding us that salvation is of God. He *chose* us, which destroys all notions of human merit. "Those who love God" were previously chosen, "the called according to His purpose," by God. We love Him because He first loved us. To God alone be the glory!

I believe everything you've just read. I believe it with all my heart. It seems that troubles would slide off me as if I were "Teflon Man," doesn't it? Unfortunately, there still appears to be a large gap between what I know to be true and how that truth works out in my life. That's the difference between head knowledge and heart knowledge, don't you think? Maybe by the end of the book I'll be able to concede that God always knows best. Maybe by then the truth will travel from the recesses of my mind to the depths of my heart.

Now, let's take a look at our second foundational text.

Hebrews 12:5-8

> You have forgotten the exhortation which speaks to you as sons: "My son, do not despise the chastening of the Lord, nor be discouraged when you are rebuked by Him; For whom the Lord loves He chastens, and scourges every son whom He receives." If you endure chastening, God deals with you as sons; for what son is there whom a father does not chasten? But if you are without chastening, of which all have become partakers, then you are illegitimate and not sons.

The subject of chastening, or discipline, is avoided by most churches today. It's easy to see why. This passage and others clearly teach that the Lord chastens all true believers. Yet when I ask in a Bible study if everyone will agree to tell us how and when they were last chastened by God, I'm met with blank stares. We can conclude only two things: *One, it's possible that we're being chastened by a loving Father but are unaware of it. Two, perhaps no chastening is taking place at the present, but has in the past or will in the future. If no chastening ever occurs, it would only prove that we're illegitimate children.* Of course, that would mean that we must be hypocrites, or pretenders to Christianity. Which is it?

We need to understand Hebrews 12 as a conclusion to Hebrews 11. The catalog of heroes of the faith cited in chapter 11 is given so that we might imitate those heroes, both in their faith and in their suffering. Hebrews 12:2 encourages us to lay aside our weights and sins that we might run our races with endurance. Does one endure happy moments or troublesome ones?

The preposterous teachings of many televangelists prove heretical in the light of Hebrews 12. Can you imagine titling a book *Your Best Life Now* and selling it in Christian bookstores? This is unfathomable unless one considers the sad state of the church today. I was browsing recently at Barnes and Noble when I spied that particular book on the top shelf at the end of the section on "religious books." The next section was labeled "true crime." It took me only a moment to move the book to the section it belonged in. Only gross biblical ignorance can account for the continued popularity of such people and their messages.

I will not spend time discussing why I believe that book's author is a heretic, but I will say that teachers who seek to focus Christians on this life rather than on the next are dangerous. Dangerous, I mean, to the poor sheep they're duping. Heaven is the next world, not this one. This world is a wilderness to be traversed. A cursory examination of the lives of Christ's closest friends would assure you that they did not expect heaven on earth. Jesus told them plainly that they would suffer, and they did. Most of the original disciples died as martyrs. Why would anyone believe that those who wrote under the inspiration of the Holy Spirit would misunderstand what Jesus was saying, while that book's author "sees" clearly. God has promised in Hebrews 12 to chasten those He loves. False teachers say that God would never do such a thing. Whom should we believe?

What weights is the writer of Hebrews alluding to? Perhaps love of this present life, worldly pleasures in excess, luxury, ease, prestige, and worldly riches? Yes, to name a few. We are to disentangle ourselves from our love of this world and its "things" that we might run faster. Let me be clear. We are not told to cast away all riches and material blessings as if they are inherently evil, but we must not trust in riches or think too highly of them. Our tendency as fallen human beings is toward inordinate affection and fondness for this present world.

Does what I just said resonate with you? Do you tend to have inordinate affection for worldly things? (That's a nice way of asking whether you love money and "stuff.") My whole stinking life has been a love affair with money. I've cheated for it, lied for it, and lost many a night's sleep over it—even since I've been a Christian! I won't go into my single-minded love for money before I became a Christian. It would sicken you. Suffice it to say that these affections took my eyes off heaven, the real prize. When earthly riches, blessings, and cares hinder my running, then I must be rid of them, because my blessings have become my burdens. *God has often chastened me through the loss of earthly goods.* Undoubtedly, ease and luxury had become too important to me. My heart's treasure was in this world, not the next. God, in fatherly love, tore ease and luxury from my hands.

Chastening, for me, has always meant pursuits by the "alphabet gangs," the I.R.S. and the F.B.I. Both agencies seem stocked with ambitious, zealous folks who, I've found, will accept the truth if they have to. I'm not surprised God often uses these agencies to chasten His people. If the Almighty ran a Craigs-list ad for "chastening agents," I'm betting twenty of the first twenty-five respondents would be agents of the government. Once they had been interviewed and discovered what "chastening" is, they'd probably volunteer to do the work for free. Yes sir, God's probably had less need to dispatch cyclones, tornadoes, and floods since the U.S. government, in its wisdom, sanctioned these agencies.

> I was never molested by any person but those who represented the state.
> —Henry David Thoreau

I'm being facetious, of course. Certainly, many nice and honorable people work for these agencies. The first forty-three I've met are probably the exceptions. I'm kidding; I've really met no more than twenty-three. A little tongue-in-cheek is okay with you, isn't it?

God has, as I said, often employed such to part me from my money. It's happened three times so far, and I doubt I've seen the last of them, because God loves me. He chastens me, the one He loves. Why? Because He's wise and my love for worldly goods is stupid. God is interested in my soul's interest.

What about you? Have you ever lost your fortune? If so, have you ever considered that God caused it to happen? Have you ever considered that God sent that spectacled little fellow with the high-pitched voice and a government ID? Listen, if he came, God sent him. Remember, even overzealous federal agents are arrows in the hand of God, the great Archer. This does not excuse unrighteous behavior by those agents, but it does remind us that God can make good use of bad behavior. Naturally, I am not saying that all government agents act wrongly, but some do. Whether they act righteously or unrighteously, however, they are still arrows in God's quiver. Have any of you, like me, loved your money a little too much? I thought so.

Sin is an impediment. Hebrews 12:1 says it easily ensnares or entangles us. We must strip off our snares. Let us lay aside all our internal and external hinderances. The Jews being addressed in Hebrews 12 had their "darling" sin, what Matthew Henry terms "an over-fondness for their own dispensation". Have you and I our "darling" sins? Whatever those "darling" sins are, they must be forsaken, as they're impeding us. When I won't willingly forsake mine, God chastens me to lighten my load. Is that your case, too?

A Christian is called to run a race of service and suffering. Not only are the saints of Hebrews 11 set forth as examples, but so is our Captain and Savior in Hebrews 12: 2. He endured the cross and despised its shame. Why? Because of "the joy that was set before Him." We are to run, suffer, and endure for the same reason. We are chastened in order that we might focus on the joy set before us.

Verse 3 requests that we compare Christ's sufferings to our own. His so exceeded ours that we should endure quietly. Now, I know I should endure suffering quietly, but I'm not very good at it. Whining, complaining, and grousing like a tired two-year-old with a too full diaper is more descriptive of my behavior under suffering.

Embarrassingly, I'm talking about the mere loss of money and perishing earthly goods, along with a reputation. It's disgusting. Christ endured real hostility to the point of shedding His blood. I've suffered very little for Christ's cause, so most of my sorry examples tend to be about worldliness, the thing that takes my heart off Christ and His service.

My propensity is to grow weary under trials and chastenings, especially when they are long and heavy. So I must remind myself to persevere, because the losses are mere earthly losses. They will come to an end either in time or at death. The rewards are eternal.

Matthew Henry, in his commentary on Hebrews 12:5, enlightens us:

> Though their enemies and persecutors may be the instruments of inflicting such sufferings on them, yet they are divine chastisements, their heavenly Father has His hand in all. . . . Those afflictions which may be truly persecutions as far as men are concerned in them are fatherly rebukes and chastisements as far as God is concerned in them.

Is the author of Hebrews saying in chapter 12 that men persecute us and treat us unfairly because they are our enemies? Yes. Is he also teaching that these persecutions from enemies are at the same time chastisements from God our Father? Yes. How can this be? Chastisements are a part of the "all things" that God makes to work together for good to those who love God. The first time I pondered this, I realized I needed to reevaluate my life. *The idea that God would chasten me was foreign to me.* My pastor had taught me that God never wanted me to suffer, not even for a moment. Yet here verse 5 was plainly contradicting my pastor. God was chastening and rebuking His sons! Verse 6 supplied the reason: "Whom the Lord loves He chastens."

My pastor and I soon parted ways, as he stubbornly declared he wouldn't serve a God who chastened His sons and daughters. He termed it child abuse. Imagine my consternation. He was making that statement while we were looking at this passage! As I said, he continued to defend his position, and I sought a new pastor.

Are God's chastenings sometimes in punishment of my sins? In a word, yes. I need only remind you of the death of David's infant by Bathsheba.

> The LORD struck the child that Uriah's wife bore to David, and it became ill. . . . It came to pass that the child died.
> (2 Samuel 12:15, 18)

Are God's chastenings always in punishment of my sins? No, sometimes they are to refine us, to separate the dross from the gold. At other times, they are to wean us from this world. We'll discuss examples of this later.

Here's the troubling part for me. If chastenings and afflictions are proofs of God's fatherly love for me, why do I dislike and even hate them? Am I really expected to be grateful when I'm chastened? Yes. Paternal kindness is, after all, paternal kindness.

The saints of all ages have one thing in common: they all have faults and follies that require correction. God, always the consummate Father, faithfully rebukes and chastens His children precisely because they *are* His children.

Remember, if you are not chastened, you must be an illegitimate child, hiding in the church, disguised as a true member.

John Calvin comments, "Why does he call those who refuse correction bastards rather than aliens? Even because he was addressing those who were members of the church."

So, is it possible that unchastened church members are merely professors and not really true believers? Yes, it is. In most cases, however, I suspect that God is chastening believers and they are simply unaware of God's promise to chasten those He loves, so His work is attributed to the devil or to chance.

We deduce that we are chastened because we are loved.

> Troubles are after all the tools by which God fashions us for better things.
> —Henry Ward Beecher

Later verses instruct us to endure the pains of chastenings wisely, judging them with an eye to our eternal good, as God does. For the present they are vexing and painful. In the end they will yield the peaceable fruit of righteousness, and in heaven we shall be grateful for all of our scourgings and chastenings. This is wisdom as only the Bible can give it. Being spiritually immature, I still fuss when the I.R.S., sickness, job loss, and other trials come trolling. How about you?

Technically, there is no such thing as a random act. There is no such thing as chance or fate. From a human perspective, events both good and bad appear to happen at random. From God's perspective, not a single event happens randomly; they are all part of God's great purpose. Now let's take a few moments to consider I Kings 22:34 from a human perspective and then from God's perspective.

1 Kings 22:34

> A certain man drew a bow at random and struck the King of Israel between the joints of his armor. So he said to the driver of his chariot, "Turn around and take me out of the battle, for I am wounded."

Israel, after King Solomon, suffered under a series of bad kings. Chief among them was Ahab. His marriage to Jezebel, daughter of a Sidonian king, only made a bad man worse. Ahab nominally worshipped the true God, but he also worshipped and served Baal, the Canaanite deity, and built a temple for Baal in Samaria. Jezebel, in turn, supported many priests and prophets of Baal. This policy of religious tolerance and idolatry angered God. (Come to think of it, it still does.)

> Ahab did more to provoke the Lord God of Israel to anger than all the kings of Israel who were before him.
> (1 Kings 16:33)

God's anger was further increased when Jezebel had Naboth murdered so her husband could obtain the vineyard he coveted. Elijah the prophet was dispatched to deliver this foreboding message:

> In the place where dogs licked the blood of Naboth, dogs shall lick your blood, even yours.
> (1 Kings 21:19)

Elijah proceeded to rebuke Ahab for making Israel sin in permitting and sponsoring Baal worship and told him that calamity would come to his home:

> Concerning Jezebel the LORD also spoke, saying, "The dogs shall eat Jezebel by the wall of Jezreel. The dogs shall eat whoever belongs to Ahab and dies in the city, and the birds of the air shall eat whoever dies in the field."
> (1 Kings 21:23-24)

Even Ahab was moved to mourn over the news. Unexpectedly, God issued a reprieve. Ahab did not return Naboth's vineyard, nor did he leave his idols, but because he outwardly humbled himself and gave glory to God, God stayed the threatened destruction of Ahab's house until the days of his sons.

Against this backdrop we come to the alliance forged between wicked King Ahab and Jehoshaphat, the good king of Judah. Ahab meditated war against Syria and asked Jehoshaphat to join with him. The pious Jehoshaphat should have known better. As Spurgeon's John Ploughman once quipped, "It's dangerous to try to lick honey off thorns."

Ahab had a standing corps of four hundred prophets. When he wished to execute a plan such as the invasion of Syria, he would, under the pretense of seeking divine approval, inquire of the prophets whether he should proceed. The prophets, seeking to please the king, would assure him of success.

I think I understand this propensity to tell the boss what he wants to hear. Doing otherwise can get you fired. I've been privy to the inner workings of a few churches (which will teach you a few things you didn't want to learn). Once, a pastor I knew quite well sequestered his elders for a night of prayer to determine whether or not the church should move from one locale to another. They prayed for an hour or so and then reassembled. All agreed that it was a poor idea to move. All felt it was wise to stay put. Did I say all? Actually, "all" didn't include the pastor, who, with his voice quivering, said, "All of you heard from the devil. God told me to move, so we will. Since you're all so unspiritual, you're fired." Some pastors and kings have a good deal in common, don't they? Weak elders and weak prophets are also brothers. Christianity is sometimes exasperating, isn't it?

Good Jehoshaphat was not satisfied and asked if a prophet of the Lord was available. Micaiah, apparently already imprisoned by Ahab, entered and after a preliminary, mocking response, delivered the message Ahab didn't want to hear. Micaiah plainly foretold that the incursion would end disastrously. The sheep would be scattered, and the shepherd killed. Believe me, Ahab realized he was the shepherd in view.

Ahab ordered Micaiah back to his cell and limited him to bread and water. Undoubtedly he intended to execute Micaiah as a false prophet upon his triumphant return from Syria. But Micaiah was unbowed, telling Ahab,

> If you ever return in peace, the LORD has not spoken by me.
> (1 Kings 22:28)

Micaiah was willing to incur a false prophet's punishment if Ahab returned alive.

Good Jehoshaphat, moved I suppose by four hundred voices against one, foolishly agreed to prosecute the war.

Ahab contrived to expose Jehoshaphat to danger and secure his own safety. The consistency of wicked men can be counted on, you know. Jehoshaphat was to wear his robes into battle, and Ahab would disguise himself as a common soldier. Pretending to do Jehoshaphat the honor of leading the army, Ahab sought only to hide himself from the Syrian soldiers. He was successful at hiding himself from the Syrians, but can a man hide himself from God?

> A certain man drew a bow at random, and struck the King of Israel between the joints of his armor. So he said to the driver of his chariot, "Turn around and take me out of the battle, for I am wounded."
> (1 Kings 22:34)

Let no man reason that he can hide from God. There was nothing random from God's viewpoint about the drawing of the bow or the shooting of the arrow. It appeared to be random to the Syrian soldier with the bow, but there was no randomness to it. God governs and directs all events. There is no such thing as a random event. No such thing as a random arrow.

Stop and consider this for a moment. Am I correct? Am I stating what the Bible teaches? If so, do you need to reconsider the "chance" happenings in your life? Is it conceivable that your life contains no "chance" happenings? Don't hurry past this. No "chance" happenings? Not one? If I'm right, then your idea about how the world really works must be completely wrong, huh?

Did the Syrian shooting the arrow realize he and his arrow were both under God's control? Remember, the Syrian wasn't a worshipper of the true God. Yet his arrow struck the right man, out of thousands, in the right place, between the joints of his armor. All praise and glory to our God!

All of these events were done by the determinate counsel and will of God. What about the events in your life? Do you need to revisit them?

Ahab lived long enough to see his army scattered, each to his own home, as Micaiah had prophesied. Ahab did not live long enough to see the prophecy of his wife's, Jezebel's, death fulfilled. But under God's direction, the dogs consumed all of Jezebel except for her skull, her feet, and the palms of her hands. After Ahab's death, his chariot was brought to the pool of Samaria to be washed. There, as Micaiah had foretold, the dogs lapped up Ahab's blood mixed with the water.

Allow me to reiterate. The Bible teaches that there never has been, nor will there ever be, a random or chance event. To us, events appear to be random, but they are not. All events are governed and directed by God Almighty. The Syrian, of his own free will, shot the arrow, it's true. It's equally true that God controlled the Syrian's being there that day, the Syrian's shooting of the arrow, and the entrance of the arrow between the joints of Ahab's armor!

Is this a new idea for you? Do you need time to digest it? Relax. That's why I wrote this little book.

His Voice is Full of Majesty

Psalm 29

The church bells of the universe
Are heard in the skies tonight,
Calling kings and angels
To witness heaven's might.

The glare of lightning fills the sky,
Joined by peals of thunder,
Reminding kings of ev'ry age
To praise the King of Wonders.

When kings fall at Christ's feet,
We see jewels in their crowns;
Swollen with earthly glory,
Kings find it hard to kneel down.

When lions roar at midnight,
All beasts are hushed and still.
So kings and angels are silenced
When God thunders from heaven's hill.

Chorus: Lightning inspires a rev'rent awe,
Thunder demands humility.
The King of Kings speaks like a King,
His voice is full of majesty.

W.D. Moore

3

Plain Talk

The church world today has little use for the idea of a sovereign God who permits the free actions of men while simultaneously governing not only those free actions but also the waves of the sea and the rising of the sun. A mechanistic view of nature and life has corroded the luster of Christ's church. It's time you and I polished the doctrines of God's sovereignty and providence so that their brilliance might once again demonstrate that they are precious jewels to God's people.

Let's begin by defining three key concepts I mentioned in the first paragraph: (1) sovereignty, (2) a mechanistic view of nature and life, and (3) providence.

Before we begin, I must take a moment to add a personal note concerning my aim in writing this little book. As always, I wish to glorify God and exalt His name among His creatures. I hope to accomplish this by learning the truths of Scripture and applying them to my life and to yours. Ezra Ministries does a thirty-minute television show called *Plain Talk about Life and the Bible*. As the name implies, I aim to be plain. There are many fine books already on the shelves regarding God and providence. Frankly, most of them are over the heads of most of our television audience. The same would be true of most of the church and parachurch Bible studies I've participated in, as well as the barroom discourses I've engaged in. Therefore, I'm directing this book at the television audience, Bible study groups, and tavern societies the Lord has graciously given me to serve.

This book is meant to be accurate but not scholarly. My desire is that it be truthful, understandable, and useful. If you cannot understand it and apply it to your life, then I will have failed. I am a layman speaking to laymen.

Recently I read a quote by a man named Ernst Rudolph, a physicist. Complaining of the ineffectiveness of physicists in making their complex theories intelligible to the general public, he said, "Any theory that cannot be easily understood by a bartender is no damn good."

I concur with this sentiment. The same is true for biblical truths. If the bartender cannot grasp what we're saying, we have failed. Have you a regular Bible study at your local pub? If not, why not? Pubs are a great place for Bible study and discussions. Invariably the bartender, waitress, or other patrons will inquire gingerly about what you're doing. I normally tell them that I'm trying to figure out how to live. A conversation about life usually ensues. Try it sometime. Starbucks is also fertile ground. I'm weary of the quarantining of biblical truths. God's truths are for the streets and alleys as well as for the Sunday school. So allow me to step down from my soapbox to reiterate that my aim is to be plain. Therefore, I will endeavor to open the beauty of God's providence to you through the lives of a few biblical figures, following a brief but needed explanation of the foundational concept of sovereignty, what is meant by the mechanistic view of nature and life, and providence.

Sovereignty

My Scribner's dictionary defines sovereignty as independent power or dominion. Scripture strongly emphasizes the independent power and dominion of God. In short, God is King. King of what, you ask? He has absolute authority over heaven, earth, and the inhabitants of heaven and earth. All God's creation and creatures are dependent on him. Pretty all-inclusive and all-encompassing, don't you think? Here are just a few related passages from the book of Psalms:

> The kingdom is the Lord's,
> and He rules over the nations.
> (Psalm 22:28)
>
> The Lord Most High is awesome;
> He is a great King over all the earth.
> (Psalm 47:2)
>
> God is the King of all the earth;
> Sing praises with understanding.
> God reigns over the nations;
> God sits on His holy throne.
> (Psalm 47:7-8)
>
> The Lord is the great God,
> And the great King above all gods. . . .
> The sea is His, for He made it;
> And His hands formed the dry land.
> Oh come, let us worship and bow down;
> Let us kneel before the Lord our Maker.
> (Psalm 95:3, 5-6)

The Bible is replete with similar declarations. God sustains all things with His almighty power and determines the ends they are destined to serve. God must, in some sense, ordain everything that comes to pass, or He's not truly sovereign. And if He's not sovereign, He's not God, right?
Is God in the details of life?

> Look at the birds of the air, for they neither sow nor reap nor gather into barns, yet your heavenly Father feeds them.
> (Matthew 6:26)

> Are not two sparrows sold for a copper coin? And not one of them falls to the ground apart from your Father's will. But the very hairs of your head are all numbered.
> (Matthew 10:29-30)

Even Ben Franklin referred to this truth when he wrote,

> I have lived, Sir, a long time, and the longer I live, the more convincing proof I see of this truth—that God governs the affairs of men. And if a sparrow cannot fall to the ground without His notice, is it probable that an empire can rise without His aid?
> —Ben Franklin

God knows everything about everything. If He knows, comprehensively, every bird that flies and falls, isn't it equally evident that He knows every gnat that lands on every cow's eyelid? If He knows the number of hairs on my old head, isn't it evident that He knows every detail of my life and the next word I'll say? Look at Matthew 10:29-30 again: "Not one of them falls to the ground apart from your Father's will." God, by His power, is sustaining the birds while they live, and they die when He wills, right? Are you and I, like the sparrows, sustained by the power of God on a moment-by-moment basis? Do we live by His power and authority until He decides it's time that we die? Yes, yes—absolutely yes! *God is, indeed, in control of* all *the details of our lives.*

Remember our first foundational Scripture verse:

> We know that all things work together for good to those who love God, to those who are the called according to His purpose.
> (Romans 8:28)

Notice that Paul is not claiming that everything that happens is good, but he is declaring the even out of the bad things that happen to us God brings good for believers. We may have confidence in our God of the details. He is working all things together for the good of believers. Pain? Suffering? Heartache? Disease? Anguish? Calamity? Persecution? Unequivocally yes. Later we'll consider some lives that demonstrate this truth, but for now, aren't you grateful He's sovereign?

Let's look at Matthew 10: 29-30 again. Do you see any room for "fate" or "chance" in "not one of them [sparrows] falls to the ground apart from your Father's will"? If God sustains the sparrows and then decides when they fall, where would chance and fate fit in? They don't. As I said in the beginning, fate and chance don't exist, except in the imaginations of unbelievers. Christianity believes in sovereignty, not fate.

The longer you reflect on this question of the extent of God's sovereignty, the more excited and humbled you'll become. Our lives, our children's lives, and our destinies are not the products of blind fate. Our God reigns. His will is coming to pass. Our lives are significant because of His care, and we are safe in His hands. Banish chance and fate from your thinking.

A Mechanistic View of Nature and Life

This error has infected the church today. Actually, the word *infected* isn't strong enough. This false view is the majority view in the church today. Like most errors, it's an old one. It's been around in various forms since Bible times. Let's see if it's your belief, too.

The mechanistic view of nature and life holds that God created the universe to run on its own. Since creation, according to this view, God has been uninvolved in the laws of nature and the lives of human beings.

The idea that God was a great watchmaker who wound the watch of creation and then left it to run by itself collides instantly with biblical Christianity. God not only creates everything, but He also sustains everything. The "normal" operations of God are what scientists term the laws of nature. They simply illustrate the standard way God governs His world. Natural laws do not operate independently of God. Does gravity exist apart from the power of God? No. God is the primary cause; gravity is the secondary cause. God exhibits His power through the real power of secondary causes, such as gravity. (We'll talk more about secondary causes later).

God sustains this world moment by moment. The world is not a giant clock running on its own power. God sustains the sun; it keeps its course because God actively wills it to. All natural laws rely on God's power. God, of course, on occasion, intervenes in this world in especially supernatural ways. We call these miracles. Consider the parting of the Red Sea, the feeding of the five thousand, and the raising of

Lazarus from the dead. Aren't these all examples of God acting "above" nature?

How is it then that this mechanistic view has gained such a foothold in the church? There are probably many reasons, but permit me to cite two obvious ones. The first reason is biblical ignorance. A casual look at the Scriptures will uncover multiple accounts of God intervening in the lives of men and women. Did Adam come into being by chance? Did David arrive at the battlefield by chance just as Goliath challenged Saul and his men? Did Jesus die on the cross by chance? Was Paul blinded by chance on the road to Damascus? As I said, biblical ignorance, which is rampant in the church today, is one reason Christians have adopted the mechanistic view of life and nature. Shame on us.

The second reason the church has been infected with this view is the prevailing desire of the church to be "relevant" to the world. This desire has allowed the world to infiltrate the church. The church and the world are like fraternal twins today. Can you imagine? The church and the world are to be at war:

> I have no use for a church which is not a church militant.
> —G. K. Chesterton

The church is to fill the world's darkness with light. For the past one hundred years, and particularly the past forty years, the roles have reversed—the darkness of the world now fills the church. One of the casualties is a belief in God's sovereignty.

If you want to have some fun and at the same time see how infected the church is today with this mechanistic view of the world, stand up in Sunday school and thank God for the storm He brought last night. You'll receive the same blank stares you'd receive if you made the same announcement at the local tavern. You will engender a discussion in both the Sunday school and the tavern, which is a fine thing. And don't be surprised if the bar patrons concede to God's sovereignty more quickly than your Sunday school classmates. The church is in a sad way today.

> We die of what we eat and drink,
> **But more we die of what we think**.
> —E. A. Robinson

Has a mechanistic view of the world become your view? Can you see how patently antibiblical it is? Good, well-meaning church members are being led astray by poor thinking. As Mr. Robinson warns above, it can be deadly — first to the parishioner, then to the parish.

A mechanistic view of the universe robs God of His sovereignty. A God who isn't sovereign is an impotent deity. An impotent deity cannot help in times of trouble, let alone *govern* times of trouble. He is barely more than a human, a creature.

> God made man in His image, and man returned the favor.
> —Voltaire

The God of the Bible is no impotent deity. He is the ruler of and over all.

My heart is awed within me,
When I think of the great miracle that still goes on,
In silence 'round me—the perpetual work
Of Thy creation, finished, yet renewed
Forever.
—W. C. Bryant

Jehovah is sovereign. He daily exerts His power to govern our world. A mechanistic worldview is a false one.

Providence

> While the term "providence" is not found in Scripture, the doctrine of providence is nevertheless eminently Scriptural.
> —Louis Berkhof

Providence refers to God's governing of the world and His care for it. The idea of providence, which is ripe with the notion that God provides for his people, is a never ending source of wonder to me as I reflect on my life. Why was I born in Springfield, Illinois? Why did I have the parents I had? Why did Ginny Roger lose interest in me in the seventh grade? Why did I suffer a severe leg injury at fifteen? How did I happen to meet my wife? How did I come to see my need of the Savior? Providence holds the answer to all of my questions—and yours. *Providence gives significance to our lives and ensures that they have meaning.*

> In Him [God] we live and move and have our being. (Acts 17:28)

> We have a necessary and constant dependence upon His providence, as the streams have upon the springs, and the beams upon the sun.
> —Matthew Henry

What breathtaking beauty—the idea that the continuance of my life is influenced and sustained by God Himself. What power and Fatherly care are in view here! Reader, put the book down and waggle your tongue. You cannot do it except by Him. Is that mind-boggling? Of course, it is. That's why I'm writing this little book. You and I owe unending thanks to God for His continual care. His goodness and wisdom are magnificent. It's good that we are under His control and care.

> All living things are living in the Hand of God. The senses see only the action of the creatures; but faith sees in everything the action of God.
> —Jean Pierre de Cassaude

A right view of providence should cure my complaining and murmuring. Do you ask, "Why me, God?" over and over? Have you noticed that this question doesn't normally follow on the heels of "good news"? Pain, loss, tragedy, and "bad news" bring on the "Why me" question. The answers are splendidly wrapped up in God's providence.

> God the great creator of all things doth uphold, direct, dispose, and govern all creatures, actions, and things, from the greatest to the least, by His most wise and holy providence.
> —*Westminster Confession of Faith,* chapter 5

Creeds are also out of favor today, but we are poorer and more ignorant for it. My grandmother Eva Moore, God rest her soul, had a poster above the door to the Sunday school when I was a boy. It said boldly, No Law but Love, No Creed but Christ. I believe my grandmother and grandfather meant well, but they were wrong in dissing creeds. If your church prides itself on not having a creed, it should be aware that it still has a creed. It's just an unwritten creed. Creed really means "belief." Which is prone to greater error and misunderstanding: a written creed or an unwritten creed? Of course, *the unwritten creed my grandmother was so proud of allowed for every church member to have his or her own creed.* If there is no clear statement of biblical doctrine in your church, it's every man for himself. Can unity possibly come from this? Can chaos be counted on to parade itself? Enough said.

Further clarification of providence and its distinguishing features will be left to the chapters ahead. It is my hope that by the end of this little book, you will find providence, as the *Westminster Confession* says, to be "to the praise of the glory of His wisdom, power, justice, goodness, and mercy."

> The world is . . . a kind of spiritual kindergarten where millions of bewildered infants are trying to spell "God" with the wrong blocks.
> —E. A. Robinson

THE CREATION OF LIGHT
And the earth was without form, and void . . . (Genesis 1: 2)

The Captain Knows What's Best for Me
Psalm 30:5
",,,weeping may endure for a night, but joy cometh in the morning."

The south winds of heaven's mercy
Are welcomed by my soul,
But a voyage of gentle breezes
Is not the captain's goal.

The north winds of adversity
Are sometimes best for me,
So the Captain steers my ship
Against the winds of mercy.

The north winds of calamity
Disturb life's placid sea.
Waves of woe cause tearful nights
As they wash over me.

The Captain charts life's course for me,
We sail where he thinks best.
North winds bring me sleepless nights,
South winds bring me rest.

Weakness and strength, wealth and want
Miseries and mercies;
The Captain steers me through life's seas,
The Captain knows what's best for me.

Chorus: Evening winds of care may howl
           But calm at mercy's dawning.
           Weeping may endure for a night,
           But joy comes in the morning.

W.D. Moore

4

A Primer on Providence

The word *primer* refers to a discussion of elementary principles or ideas. Laymen like me, I've discovered, typically learn more quickly by discussion than by straightforward lecture, whether oral or written. Therefore, I've opted to begin this chapter with a list of questions that I hope will open our eyes, minds, and hearts to the expanse contained in the simple idea of providence.

MIT physics professor Walter Lewin, also known as the "Physics Magician," responded to an interviewer's question by saying, "What counts is not what you cover, but what you uncover." The truth of that statement applies to any subject, including ours. One question regarding providence and its explanation necessarily leads to another as the richness and fullness of the concept begins to sink in. So, let's get on with the questions.

For Further Consideration

1. Are you saying that God can look into the future and *see* whom I will meet next, or do you believe that God actually *arranges* whom I will meet next?

2. What gives God the right to rule over me?

3. What about sickness? Isn't most of it caused by tiny microorganisms rather than by God?

4. How can my cancer diagnosis be a good thing?

5. How can God bring good out of tragedy?

6. If God controls everything, why does He permit wicked people to prosper?

***

Now, if you're ready, let's look at these questions one at a time.

***1. Are you saying that God can look into the future and* see *whom I will meet next, or do you believe that God actually* arranges *whom I will meet next?*

Let's begin to answer that question with a quotation from John Calvin:

> Let the reader remember that the providence we mean is not one by which the Deity, sitting idly in Heaven, looks on at what is taking place in the world, but one by which He, as it were, holds the

helm, and overrules all events. Hence His providence extends not less to the hand than to the eye. That is to say, He not only sees, but ordains what He wills to be done.

If God only watched as things happened but knew in advance that they *would* happen, most folks would be comfortable with the idea. But God does much more than just watch, and the fact of His active involvement in our destinies is what makes most people uncomfortable. We like to be in charge of our own destinies. In a word, we want to be sovereign. Unfortunately for us, the job of sovereign in our lives is already filled by God. And since that position is taken, we're left with the position of subjects. Subjects have freedom, but it is a limited freedom. What limits it, you ask? Better to ask *who* limits it. My freedom is limited by my Sovereign, of course. How reasonable! The life of subjects is an orderly one. The Sovereign sets boundaries to how far His subjects may go. He gives them responsibilities, work to do, food to eat, quarters to live in, etc. My Sovereign and yours does all of this for us and always has, even if I didn't realize it for forty years.

R. C. Sproul once wrote that God not only "looked on," but He "looked *after*" us. I'm glad that's true. God is actively directing, establishing, and ruling all of our lives, and He is no mere spectator. John Calvin said that God's providence "extends not less to the hand than to the eye." And Sproul astutely points out that God not only "watches us" but also "*watches over*" us. His hand is active in our lives.

So God doesn't just foresee whom you will meet in the future; He foreordains whom you will meet in the future.

Did Moses fall into the hands of Pharaoh's daughter by accident? Was Joseph sold to traders on the way to Egypt by accident? Was David born into Jesse's family by accident? Was Jesus born of Mary by accident? Were you born of your mother by accident? Staggering, isn't it?

Any chance there's anything chance about whom you'll meet tomorrow?

> **Is your place a small place?**
> Tend it with care!
> He set you there.
>
> **If your place a large place?**
> Guard it with care!
> He set you there.
>
> **Whatever your place, it is**
> Not yours alone, but His,
> Who set you there.
> (Anonymous)

2. What gives God the right to rule over me?

Again, let's begin our discussion with a couple of quotations:

> In the beginning God created the heavens and the earth.
> (Genesis 1:1)

> God said, "Let Us make man in Our image, according to Our likeness; let them have dominion over the fish

of the sea, over the birds of the air, over the cattle, over all the earth and over every creeping thing that creeps on the earth."
(Genesis 1:26)

From the beginning the order was established: Creator on the left and creature on the right. One Creator, eternal in nature, and many creatures, dependent in nature. One Sovereign with many subjects. What is your answer when your children ask defiantly, "What gives you the right to tell me what to do?" The correct answer is, "God has the right to rule over His creation, and He has given me the right as your parent to tell you what to do."

It is probably time for me to remind you of a fact that keeps getting lost in the church today. *Life is not about you.* I repeat, *your life is not about you.* It *is* all about number one, but *you* are *not* number one. *God* is. All of history is, indeed, *His* story. Romans 8:28 ends by saying that "all things work together for good to those who love God, to those who are the called according to His purpose." *His purpose.* God's purpose has always been, and continues to be, to glorify Himself in the redemption of hopelessly wicked but repentant, born-again believers. He will also glorify Himself in the judgment and eternal punishment of wicked but unrepentant unbelievers. History, *His story*, is all about Him, His purpose, and His glory. God remains on the stage during the whole production. You and I enter stage right, dance a soft-shoe for a moment, and exit stage left. The play is not about us; it's about Him.

We have significance only because He says we do. No wonder He rules over us. He's the great Original—you're not, and neither am I:

> "I am the Alpha and the Omega, the Beginning and the End," says the Lord.
> (Revelation 1:8)

If the angels gladly submit to His glorious rule, why the reluctance on my part and yours? There must be something wrong in our thinking.

> Like a pilot [God] steers the ship of the whole creation.
> —Thomas Watson

History is about the Pilot, not the scalawags and the crew.

3. What about sickness? Isn't most of it caused by tiny microorganisms rather than by God?

Science has proved that microorganisms are the cause of many and varied diseases. The real question is, do those microorganisms act independently, or are they, too, under God's control?

We refer to microorganisms as second causes (more on this later, I promise). They do act to cause sickness. But they do not act independently. God, the first cause, "doth uphold, direct, dispose, and govern all creatures, actions, and things, from the greatest even to the least" (*Westminster Confession of Faith,* chapter 5, section 1).

I believe the *Westminster Confession* has correctly captured the Bible's position regarding the extent of God's control over His world. "From the greatest even to the least," the Confession says. In your estimation, would microorganisms fall under "the least"?

> All things are without exception fully controlled—despite all appearances to the contrary.
> —Philip E. Hughes

Nothing eludes God's eye or hand. The microorganism invading your body as well as the gene you inherit that causes blindness are both under His control. Likewise ruled are the Republican Party presidential nominee's selection and the fall of the Roman Empire.

> Who has made man's mouth? Or who makes the mute, the deaf, and seeing, or the blind? Have not I, the LORD?
> (Exodus 4:11)

Yes, of course there are immediate causes of disease, such as microorganisms and genes, but behind them all is the sovereign purpose of God.

If you're beginning to be convinced that God controls even tiny microorganisms, then you probably want to ask why His control of them ends in your becoming ill, right? Let's up the ante and move on to the next question.

4. How can my cancer diagnosis be a good thing?

First, we must be agreed that God not only is *able* to control cancers but actually does so. Remember, "all things," great and small, life-giving and life-taking, are under His control. Before I answer question 4 directly, please consider this with me: Is God infinitely wise? Is God infinitely good? Is God infinitely powerful? If you agree that He's all three—and unchangeably so—we can move on.

Can an infinitely powerful, infinitely good, and infinitely wise God ever *make a mistake or do an unwise thing?* We're agreed that He makes no unwise decisions, correct? Okay, then, it must be wise for God to permit the sickness-bearing microorganisms as well as the cancer gene to exist. If our wise God felt it were better that they didn't exist, He would have the power to do away with them permanently, wouldn't He? Therefore, it seems best to me to conclude that if illness-bearing microorganisms as well as cancers exist, it is because the ever-wise, ever-good, and ever-powerful Deity has permitted them to exist.

Question 4 is one step farther down logic's road. How can anyone's getting cancer be a good thing? I'm tempted to tell you the story of a local man who died as I was writing this book. I want to tell you of the profound changes that occurred in him and in the rest of his family during his months of suffering before his death. I would like to detail the consideration that he gave to his soul's interest. Consideration he had precious little time for before his diagnosis. Perhaps I will later. For now, I want to remind you of one of this book's foundational Scripture verses:

> We know that all things work together for good to those who love God, to those who are the called according to His purpose.
> (Romans 8:28)

Does cancer fall under the category of "all things"? Then the real question is how does God make cancer, a bad thing, work for good? Please note again, first, that this promise applies only to those who are "called according to His purpose." That is, only born-again Christians are in view. Unbelievers have no reason to think a diagnosis of cancer will work to their good unless it causes them to face their own fragility, as it often does.

> **Joy makes a man love this cold world,**
> of time, and sins, and sod,
> But sorrow sets its hopes upon
> Eternity and God.
> —Horace C. Carlisle

On the other hand, true believers should be heartened by the verse's assertion that "all things"—even cancer—will work together for their good. God cannot lie.

You asked "how can," and I hinted at one of the answers in my brief account of the local man who died. *His* cancer caused *him* to realize *his* mortality. His cancer caused him to ponder death, the causes of it, and the certainty of it. His cancer ultimately benefited his soul. His cancer piloted his family members to the same considerations. Their souls benefited. I'd say his cancer worked for good, wouldn't you? I'd say his cancer, thanks to the Almighty, became a "good thing."

Thoreau said that many people can date a profound change in their lives from the reading of some particular book. I believe he was right. People can also date profound changes to particular conversations, ones that are indelibly etched into their memories.

Beverly Marshall, my friend Artie's wife, and I had one such conversation. Beverly suffered from cancer in her twenties and as a result was unable to bear children. But God blessed her through her three adopted children. Lindsey, Leslie, and Andrew would know Bev's loving influence through the years. Through the years, Bev bore her pain gallantly. Growing accustomed to her abiding pain caused her to lose her life. When I feel pain, I take notice, as I've lived a mostly pain-free life. But although Bev took note of her heightened pain, she later told me, she did not look into the reason for it. Pain was Bev's constant companion, so its increased intensity did not send her scurrying to the doctor as it would have another person.

By the time Bev's new tumor was discovered, it had grown to frightening proportions and the cancer had metastasized. Treatment proved unfruitful. Bev's weight dropped into the mid-eighties. Artie and the children stood by her valiantly, but Death was pacing up and down Lucerne Street, waiting for God's permission to enter #14.

As I drove to Bev's home, I asked what you're asking: *How can getting cancer be a good thing?*

"Artie, go upstairs a minute and let me talk to Bill, will you?" Bev asked, when I arrived. Artie, his eyes brimming with tears, complied.

"Billy, they say I've got three months to live."

"They've lied to you," I replied.

"What do you mean?"

"I don't know how you can last three months. Your color is bad. I'm no doctor, but two weeks seems more likely. Are you eating?"

"Not much. Thanks, I want you to be truthful. I don't think it will be long either."

"Bev, you mad at God?"

"Why would I be?"

"Andrew's such a little guy, and he's losing the mother he just got. I thought it might make you question God's goodness."

"Billy, God's been so good to me. He's taken such good care of me; I know He'll take care of Andrew, too."

"Wow! You blow me away. I thought I might have to remind you that He's good. Now *you've* reminded *me*."

"Billy, do me a favor. If I start to complain during these next two weeks, stop me. God has been so good to me: it'd be wrong for me to complain, and I'm getting ready to see Him face-to-face."

I couldn't speak. I just looked into those weary, pained eyes and smiled. What I saw was Christianity at its finest. That conversation with my friend Bev caused me to take stock of my stand for Christ. I reconsecrated myself, and my heart has had eyes for heaven ever since. Bev's cancer was a good thing for me as well as for her. God made it work for my own soul's good.

Bev slipped through Artie's arms and into her Savior's about ten days later. Do you think Bev's cancer drew her heart closer to her Lord? Anything that brings greater closeness to Christ is good. Bev's body suffered, but her soul prospered.

5. How can God bring good out of tragedy?

The same question challenged me twenty years ago. The tragedy I have in mind was a very personal one. I immediately dispatched a fax to my then-new friend Dr. John Gerstner. As I noted earlier, his return fax stated, in essence, "Mr. Moore, yours was not a tragedy. No believer has a tragedy. God makes all things work together for your good. There are no exceptions. A tragedy is anything, good or bad, that happens to an unbeliever."

That is not an exact quote, but it is close. Dr. Gerstner's answer did not satisfy me at the time, but today I see the truthfulness and wisdom of it.

That it was *my* tragedy wasn't lost on Dr. Gerstner, but he was bound to remind me of the biblical truth I'm reminding you of in this little book. *All things* work together for good for Christians. God makes it so.

Did you catch his last sentence? He felt compelled to complete my education. For an unbeliever, even winning the lottery is a tragedy. What!? Adding a pile of money to an unredeemed sinner's arsenal can do his soul no good. Remember, we need to judge all things to be good or bad according to whether they promote or injure our soul's best interest. Everything else in life is relatively inconsequential. Good news is good only if it benefits your soul.

A short while ago, I learned of an atheistic family that lost its young father to an auto accident. Without question, the death of a spouse at age twenty-three is a tragedy for an unbeliever. The children lose their father, and the wife her best friend. What is more dispiriting than this: a grandfather outliving his son? It's especially sad because no comfort can be received from a God you don't believe in. Indeed, both good news and bad news are bad news for an unbeliever. But God is able even to make the death of a spouse early in life to work for a believer's good.

Dr. Gerstner is right on both points. Any event, whether seemingly good or bad, that happens to an unbeliever is a tragedy. Conversely, there is not a single thing that can happen in the life of a believer that doesn't work, by God's power and grace, for his good, including the desertion of a spouse or the loss of a job. Later we'll look at some examples from history. Don't misunderstand me; I'm *not* saying that backing out of your driveway and running over your three-year-old is inherently good. Neither was Bev's cancer or the loss of my daughter's leg. Gut-wrenching pain and agony are involved. However, I *am* saying that believers and only believers have God's assurance that He will make *all things* work together for good for those who love Him and are called according to His purpose. I say this to you tenderly if you're presently suffering, because it's true.

> **Sweet are the uses of adversity**
> Which, like the toad, ugly and venomous,
> Wears yet a precious jewel in his head.
> —William Shakespeare

6. OK, then, if God controls everything, why does He permit wicked people to prosper?

Prosper in this world, you mean? The prosperity of wicked people is limited to this world. Prosperity in the next world, the eternal world, is limited to Christians and is what Christians live for, right?

In chapter 1 you met the rich man of Luke 16, along with his neighbor, Lazarus, the beggar. The rich man lived sumptuously while Lazarus suffered, begged for crumbs, and had the dogs lick his sores.

The prosperity the gentleman achieved in this world was probably the envy of his neighbors. No one envied Lazarus. Neighbors can be shortsighted. Am I? Are you? Prosperity here for a day, or prosperity in heaven for eternity: What sort of choice is that? *Rich unbelievers deserve pity, not envy.* We are so earthly minded and worldly that this subject is difficult for us—at least it is for me. Your question about prosperity was my own question. It prompted me to write another little book, *Wallowing in the World: A Peek at Earthly Mindedness*, to remind me of the foolishness of worrying about the prosperity of the wicked and the deceitfulness of riches.

> The Pharisees made a jest of Christ's sermon against worldliness; now this parable was intended to make those mockers serious. The tendency of the gospel of Christ is both to reconcile us to poverty and affliction and to arm

us against temptations to worldliness and sensuality.
—Matthew Henry

The great curtain is being drawn back in this parable to give us a peek into the next world *before* we enter that world at death. There is often such a great difference between the lifestyles and estates of wicked rich men and godly poor men in this world that many godly people have been perplexed about it through the ages. Even the psalmist Asaph struggled with the idea:

> As for me, my feet had almost stumbled;
> My steps had nearly slipped.
> For I was envious of the boastful,
> When I saw the prosperity of the wicked. . . .
> They are not in trouble like other men,
> Nor are they plagued like other men. . . .
> Violence covers them like a garment.
> Their eyes bulge with abundance; . . .
> Who are always at ease;
> They increase in riches. . . .
> When I thought how to understand this,
> It was too painful for me—
> Until I went into the sanctuary of God;
> Then I understood their end. . . .
> Oh how they are brought to desolation in a moment!
> They are utterly consumed with terrors.
> (Psalm 73:2-3, 5-7, 12, 16-17, 19)

The psalmist found the cure for his bewilderment. He considered the end of the wicked rich man. To be brought into desolation in a moment and to be consumed with terrors is a horrifying end to a short life.

> Do not fret because of evildoers,
>   Nor be envious of the workers of iniquity.
> For they shall soon be cut down like the grass. . . .
>   Do not fret because of him who prospers in his way,
>   Because of the man who brings wicked schemes to pass. . . .
> For yet a little while and the wicked shall be no more.
> (Psalm 37:1-2, 7, 10)

David penned this perceptive psalm, in which he urges us twice not to fret. Why? Because life is short. Consider the end of the wicked rich man.

God sovereignly governs the lives of unbelievers as well as those of believers. In Psalm 73, God is said to set them in slippery places. Unbelievers poorly reckon how slippery their perch in this world is. We must not fret or be shortsighted. Mistake it not—God is governing the entirety of His world.

The rich man in Luke 16 had his "good things" in this world for but a terribly short time. Lazarus had his "good things" for eternity. I reiterate, pity rich unbelievers. Do not think of envying them. James 5:5 echoes this sentiment:

> You have lived on the earth in pleasure and luxury; you have fattened your hearts as in a day of slaughter.

5

Jumping into the Deep End
Concurrence and Humanity's Freedom

About now you may be wondering why I would introduce *concurrence* into our discussion when it's a term very few people know. Well, some terms confuse the issue, but others bring order and light. *Concurrence* is one of the latter. If the concept of concurrence weren't crucial to our understanding of providence, I would not expose you to it—I promise. So buckle up and stay with me, Lazybones.

When two or three streams or rivers flow together and become one, we call it a confluence (a flowing together). The synonym for confluence is concurrence. It may be helpful to think of it in terms of simultaneous occurrences. In our case, we are thinking of God's actions flowing simultaneously with our human actions.

With regard to historical events, we can see that God was acting through human deeds to bring about His plan. The very humans performing the deeds were often unaware they were acting at God's behest. As far as they were concerned, they were freely doing what they wanted to do. Peter gives us a prime example of this:

> Men of Israel, hear these words: Jesus of Nazareth, a man attested by God to you by miracles, wonders, and signs which God did through Him in your midst,

> as you yourselves also know—Him being delivered by the determined purpose of God, you have taken by lawless hands, have crucified, and put to death. (Acts 2:23)

The most important event in history, the crucifixion of Christ, is a clear example of concurrence. His death is first an act of God: "Him being delivered by the determined purpose of God." His death is second an act committed by wicked men: "You have taken by lawless hands, have crucified, and put to death." These two parties, God and the wicked men, were acting simultaneously and with different ends in mind. Yet God was governing it all, wasn't He?

Did the wicked men have any clue that they were executing God's plan? No. As far as they were concerned, they were executing their own plan. Were they guilty of the greatest crime in history? Yes. Peter terms it "taken by lawless hands." Were these men guilty of murder? Yes, and it was the murder of an innocent man. Now here's the key question: *Did God desire that Jesus be crucified?* Yes. It occurred precisely *as* God had planned and precisely *when* He had planned it. One party, God, had a righteous plan, the redemption of sinful men. The other party, wicked men, had an unrighteous plan, the murder of an innocent man. Can you see that this is a clear example of concurrence? Concurrence isn't as difficult to understand as you had feared.

Could the men have crucified Jesus a day earlier? No. God governed the actions of everyone in the drama so that it would happen exactly when it did. Could the wicked men have beaten Jesus to death instead of crucifying him? No. God had ordained long before that Jesus would be crucified:

> Dogs have surrounded Me;
> The congregation of the wicked has enclosed Me.
> They pierced My hands and My feet;
> I can count all My bones.
> They look and stare at Me.
> They divide My garments among them.
> And for My clothing they cast lots.
> (Psalm 22:16-18)

This was written nearly a thousand years before the day of Jesus' crucifixion.

> I gave my back to those who struck Me,
> and My cheeks to those who plucked out the beard;
> I did not hide My face from shame and spitting.
> (Isaiah 50:6)

> He was despised and rejected by men,
> A Man of sorrows and acquainted with grief. . . .
> Yet we esteemed Him stricken,
> Smitten by God, and afflicted. . . .
> And the LORD has laid on Him the iniquity of us all.
> (Isaiah 53:3-4, 6)

Again, Isaiah lived nearly eight hundred years before Jesus' death.

Is there any doubt that the men surrounding the cross acted freely and wickedly? Is there any doubt that God governed these wicked actions? In this case, God appointed that Jesus would die on that exact afternoon to save His people. God permitted the wicked men to do what they wanted to in order to fulfill His plan. This, my friends, is concurrence.

> There's a divinity that shapes our ends,
> Rough-hew them as we will.
> —William Shakespeare's *Hamlet*

The wicked men acted freely and accomplished what they wanted. God acted freely and accomplished what He had planned all along. God's sovereign plan transcended the plan of the wicked men. God's sovereignty is established plainly here and in the lives of many others, including Esther, Jephthah, Moses, and Joseph.

Now our task is to apply this understanding to our own lives. Can a group of thugs determine to kill you tonight? Yes. Can they kill you if God does not permit them to? No. Could God stop all killing if He wanted to? Yes. Why doesn't He? Sometimes God thwarts the murderous plans of wicked people. Other times, God permits wicked people to do wicked things because it's part of His plan. *What!?* God's purpose and will are hidden from us concerning the working out of history. After all, it is, as I said before, *His* story.

> Woe to him who strives with his Maker!
> Let the potsherd strive with the potsherds of the earth!
> Shall the clay say to him who forms it, "What are you making?"
> (Isaiah 45:9)

Every big decision you've made in your life you have made freely, but God had all those decisions, good and bad, righteous or unrighteous, in His plan. It is equally true of all the small, seemingly insignificant decisions in our lives. God sovereignly ordains whatsoever comes to pass. *Whew!*

Take a moment to reflect on your life up to this point. If you are a believer, ask yourself if you could have died before the day you were converted. Well? Could you have been the victim of the murderous thugs I mentioned earlier? No, their plans would have come to naught, because God had already determined that you would be converted at the exact moment you were. Would the thugs' have had any awareness that God was keeping them from killing you? No, they would have blamed their failure on car trouble, a gun that jammed, your noticing the thugs out of the corner of your eye, or whatever other reason occurred to them. (Remember, the title of this chapter warned you that we were jumping into the deep end.)

We're going to again consider some questions to aid us in our understanding of the ways of our awesome God. But before we do, allow me to relate a more recent tale that will provide further evidence for this principle of concurrence.

The friends, passing the joint back and forth at the Sixty-Six Drive-In, laughed raucously at Peter Sellers on the big outdoor screen as he bungled his way through another *Pink Panther* Inspector Clouseau investigation. The backseat was littered with crumpled Schlitz Beer cans.

The movie ended, and the cars filed noisily, one behind another, toward the single-lane exit. Dave, the driver, suddenly slammed on his brakes, setting off an unholy chorus of auto horns. The friends just sat there, sharing another joint and laughing.

The pounding on the window interrupted them. The fool in the El Camino directly behind the friends was now filling the air with invectives. Dave rolled the driver's window down and hissed a response that I will not repeat. As they drove away, the friends congratulated themselves for causing such a disturbance.

A few blocks later, the El Camino pulled alongside them. The driver, a sort of Robert Blake look-alike from Truman Capote's *In Cold Blood,* shouted, "Pull over! Pull over!"

Dave, never one to back down from a fight, looked for a place that would draw the fewest onlookers.

Dave's passenger offered, "Forget it, Dave, I'm hungry. Forget this fool."

Dave gunned the three forty-eight, and the El Camino fool was left shouting at no one.

Two new beers were cracked and the friends' normal conversation renewed over whether they would hit the Sazerac bar for chili or the Jack Robinson System for a burger? The two nineteen-year-olds lived for joints, beer, grub, and girls. Before a decision on where to eat could be reached or a conversation about girls could begin, the El Camino again roared alongside. Now both the original fool and his passenger were shouting threats.

Dave calmly reached beneath his seat for a concealed silver-plated pistol. As he took aim, the El Camino sped off. Apparently, the driver's bravado did not extend to gunfights. But Dave gave chase. The pursuit went down North Grand Avenue to North Fifth Street. A quick left by the El Camino failed to shake Dave. The El Camino slid into a yard on the left, just across the railroad tracks. The fool and his passenger spilled out even before the El Camino had fully stopped.

Two shots rang out from Dave's gun. Dave's passenger could not tell whether either bullet found its target, but he did see the flashing gumball lights come to life in the car immediately trailing Dave's.

"What should I do?" Dave rasped. "This is Senator Horsley's pistol, from the burglary!"

"Give me the gun!"

Dave passed it faster than he'd been passing the joints all night. One heave sent the pistol airborne across the roof of the car and up into the blackened row of homes.

The friends were forced off the road and into the schoolyard by the pursuing officer. Dave's car was soon ringed by squad cars, bulging, it seemed, with gun-wielding deputies.

Both Dave and his passenger hoped the shots had missed the fool and his passenger. The friends surrendered and were restrained, and then a search for the gun commenced. Two hours of scouring the neighborhood by the deputies failed to produce the weapon. The friends were released pending the discovery of the pistol. Both shots had missed, so without the gun, there was really no crime.

The friends rejoiced as only two imbecilic, worthless boys can. After a bowl of chili at the Sazerac, they returned and began a search for the pistol.

As daybreak approached, they gave up. These friends had no understanding of providence, so they could not appreciate what God had done for them. They did not understand how the world really works.

As you've probably guessed by now, I was Dave's passenger. Life for us, was one endless crime spree. Most were petty; some were not. *I had no idea that the God I thought didn't exist was watching over me and watching after me.*

God wasn't finished. One week later, as I manned the counter at the pool hall, a stranger paused as he reached the top stair.

"Need something?" I growled. He glared nervously in all directions and motioned me closer.

"Know anybody who wants to buy a gun?" he whispered.

"What type?"

"Here it is." The stranger pulled his jacket open to reveal a shiny, silver-plated pistol. It was Senator Horsley's.

Needless to say, I bought it without even hinting at negotiating the price. Turns out the guy lived on North Fifth Street and had rushed outside to see what all the commotion was about. My heave had sent the pistol skittering right up the stranger's driveway. It had come to rest in plain view, directly beneath the security light. The stranger had quickly scooped it up and scampered inside. He lied to the police when they knocked, made a few hundred dollars for himself, and saved Dave and me a stretch in prison.

Had I understood providence, I would have fallen to my knees in awe. In my ignorance, I drove to the lake to rid myself of the gun and returned to being a worthless imbecile. I did not understand how the world really worked.

Consider what happened: Dave and I had acted wickedly throughout. The fool and his friend in the El Camino also exhibited no redeeming qualities. The stranger? He committed at least three felonies. We all did what we wanted. We all acted freely. We all had no idea that God was involved. God governed all of the free actions of these pathetic patsies. Now you know why I insist you learn about concurrence. Was it all a set of "random" events or coincidences? Of course not. God was working out His purpose through imbeciles and fools. Before time began, God decided to redeem at least one of those fools—me. The stranger delivered the pistol freely to me at the pool hall. The stranger had no idea God was using him to deliver the gun to me. Why would God do that? Because He could. Because He knew the day would come when I would understand providence and what He'd done for me. And because God wants *you* to understand what providence is so that you might take another look at your own life. Slip on your glasses with the providence lenses, take a look at your life, and see how the world really works.

For Further Consideration

1. If what you say is true, then weren't the wicked men around the cross just puppets?

2. Is it correct to think of concurrence as two mules pulling together, each doing his part (something like a joint effort)?

3. Are you saying that God doesn't just endow me with energy in a general way but actually energizes me to specific actions?

4. When, exactly, do I operate independently of the will and power of God?

5. If you're right, doesn't that make God responsible for my sin?

6. In a nutshell, are you saying that while I'm ordering a caramel latte at Starbucks, God is acting in and through me to work out His own plan?

7. Isn't it a contradiction to say that people are free *and* God is sovereign?

***

1. If what you say is true, then weren't the wicked men around the cross just puppets?

At first blush it might seem so, but we should not leap to that conclusion. The Bible clearly teaches that the providence of God extends to the actions of human beings. *They do act freely, but not independently of the will of God.*

> The LORD said to Joshua, "Do not be afraid because of them, for tomorrow about this time, *I will deliver all of them slain* before Israel. You shall hamstring their horses and burn their chariots with fire." So Joshua and all the people of war with him came against them . . . and they attacked them. And the LORD delivered them into the hand of Israel.
> (Joshua 11:6-8, emphasis added)

Did the Lord work out His plan? Did God insure victory? Did Joshua and his soldiers fight? Yes, yes, and yes. Did God appear to them visibly? Of course not. Nevertheless, God did deliver the enemy slain. That day, would it appear that Joshua delivered them? Yes, and he, in fact, did. However, above all, God delivered them. The deliverance was part of God's plan. Neither the men around the cross nor Joshua's men were puppets, but they were under God's control.

What if your life actually works this way? *What if you act freely but God governs your actions at the same time?* I assure you, that is precisely how your life works. Now you can see why I said at the beginning that it is impossible to understand your life if you don't understand providence.

In *Matthias at the Door,* written by E. A. Robinson, a sad character named Timberlake says to Natalie, an equally sad character, that Matthias, the story's primary character, had some holes torn "in the rich web of his complacency," letting some truths come in. Whether Matthias would see the truth or would see only holes was the question. The truth about God's providence in your life is the key to understanding your past, present, and future. Will you see the truth or only the holes?

I also told you that this was the deep end. Take a moment to ponder all this and catch your breath.
God is completely in charge of His world.

> The King's heart is in the hand of the LORD,
> Like the rivers of water;
> He turns it wherever He wishes.
> (Proverbs 21:1)
>
> You shall remember the LORD your God, for it is He who gives you power to get wealth.
> (Deuteronomy 8:18)

The King does what he wants? Yes. God, at the same time, is turning the King's heart? Yes.

The wealth I've accumulated: God gave it to me? Yes. But I thought it was a result of my hard work and wise dealings. It is. You work diligently, and God makes the work profitable. This is simply amazing. You may object, at this point, that you've never understood the world this way. Well, should we alter the truth because you didn't understand it? Or will you allow the Bible to correct your thinking? The choice is yours, and it's foolish to think that your view of how the world works is superior to God's. *Christians do, indeed, have a peculiar understanding of the world. It's also accurate.*

We all applaud people who are wise enough and strong enough to change their views when the evidence demands it.

We all, also, find that changing our views is a difficult thing to do because of our pride.

> When the facts change, I change my mind. What do you do, Sir?
> —John Maynard Keynes

The renowned economist had to change his position a few times after receiving new information. What about you?

2. Is it correct to think of concurrence as two mules pulling together, each doing his part (something like a joint effort)?

Nice try, but no. Each action in its entirety is both a deed of man and a deed of God. For example, I'm writing this sentence by my own hand because I want to. No one, especially God, is forcing me to write just now. I could take a walk, eat some "Cherry Garcia" ice cream, phone my wife to remind her how thoroughly I adore her, or simply take a nap. But it would be a mistake to think that God isn't governing my writing. I am writing freely, because I wish to. It is equally true that God freely governs my writing. But, it is not a joint effort; it is my effort. Yet God permits me to write, doesn't He? God may even have prompted me to write, correct? Could he stop me from writing one more word? Of course. The power of life and death lies in His hands:

> The LORD kills and makes alive;
> He brings down to the grave and brings up.
> (I Samuel 2:6)

My very breath is dependent on His will.

My writing today as well as the birth of the Himalayan Mountain Goat's calf are both under God's control and government. God is omnipotent. This does not tell us how God controls all things, but it does evidence that He can do whatever He wants, whenever He wants:

> All the inhabitants of the earth are reputed as nothing;
> He does according to His will in the army of Heaven
> And among the inhabitants of the earth.
> No one can restrain His hand
> Or say to Him, "What have you done?"
> (Daniel 4:35)

> Whatever the LORD pleases, He does,
> In heaven and in earth. . . .
> He makes lightning for the rain;
> He brings the wind out of His treasuries.
> (Psalm 135: 6-7)

> We have obtained an inheritance, being predestined according to the purpose of Him who works all things according to the counsel of His will.
> (Ephesians 1:11)

No one restrains God. He does what He pleases. He works all things "according to the counsel of His will." Does this sound like two mules working together? This should stop you in your tracks. Is it possible you and I have a much lower view of God than we should? May God forgive us.

Unable as I am to fathom it, Ephesians 1:11 is correct—God "works *all things* according to the counsel of His will" (emphasis added). God governs His world in a hands-on fashion without forcing me to do anything against my will. But I must emphasize that there is no room for the idea that two mules, harnessed together, equally sharing the load, accurately portrays concurrence. Each man freely does what he wants. *God easily governs all people so that they and their actions glorify Him.*

Don't tell me you have a headache. Remember, we are to seek understanding more than silver or hidden treasure. Finding silver or hidden treasure requires sacrifice and hard work, right? Since understanding is more precious than silver or hidden treasure, you'd expect a headache or two to acquire it, wouldn't you? Fix a hot toddy with a Dramamine and Aspirin chaser and read on.

This is heady stuff. I press this issue primarily because of previous experience. At some point in a discussion of providence, we humans tend to form the idea that we are sort of equal partners with God. This tendency to humanize God and deify ourselves leads us to an improper view of providence.

Conversely, I am trying to avoid the error I mentioned earlier of settling for a mechanistic view of the world. God did not just wind up the old watch and withdraw to watch it run on its own. God initiates or permits *all* that comes to pass. A mechanical view of the world is at its heart merciless; the fates are not only blind and heartless: they are also irrelevant. Nothing is independent of the divine will.

> The work of God always has the priority, for a man is dependent on God in all that he does. The statement of Scripture, "Without me you can do nothing," applies in every field of endeavor.

—Louis Berkhof

3. Are you saying that God doesn't just endow me with energy in a general way but actually energizes me to specific actions?

Congratulations! You deserve the junior theologian's badge. That's exactly what I'm saying. There is no absolute principle of self-activity in you to which God joins His activity. Your impulse to action proceeds from God. Surprised? Awed?

Does God cause everything in nature to work and move in the direction of a predetermined outcome? Yes. Is that difficult to understand? Of course. I confess I nearly had a stroke the first time I learned of this. I disliked the idea and felt certain it couldn't be biblical. But I was mistaken. I had to change my thinking about the way God governs His world.

> Everyone's entitled to his own opinion, but no one's entitled to his own facts.
> —Daniel Patrick Moynihan

The former New York Senator was very astute. The Bible manifests a sovereign God who is working out His plan. We are acting freely, but He is governing our actions, good and bad, for His own ends. That I didn't recognize this for forty years never altered the facts. I had my opinion, but I didn't have the facts. The same is true for you. You and I need to catch up with God's unchangeable wisdom. Our own wisdom is nothing. It's a good thing God gave us the Bible, huh?

> There are diversities of activities, but it is the same God who works all in all.
> (I Corinthians 12:6)

> Work out your own salvation with fear and trembling; for it is God who works in you both to will and to do for His good pleasure.
> (Philippians 2:13)

Human effort is what God commands and uses to achieve His purpose. Our wills and actions are the very areas where God's own power works.

4. *When, exactly, do I operate independently of the will and power of God?*

Does "never" satisfy you? None of the moments in your life is independent of God's will and power,

> for in Him we live and move and have our being.
> (Acts 17:28)

Divine activity accompanies all your actions and mine. Let's go back to my writing of this book. As my pen moves along the paper, *divine activity is involved, but without robbing me of my freedom.* The writing is mine. The action of writing is mine. My action is free. That's why I'm held responsible for what I write. If I teach you incorrectly, I have sinned; God hasn't sinned. Yet divine activity is involved even in my act of sinning. When I teach incorrectly, God knowingly permits me to do so. He could stop me but chooses not to. Even when I'm sinning, I do not operate independently of the will and power of God. Let me be plain: *God does not sin, nor is He capable of sin.* Heaven forbid you should misunderstand me to that extent. But even if I do write and sin, God is actively in it.

Remember, in Him we live and move and have our being. We are free but dependent. Only God is truly independent. More on this later.

5. If you're right, doesn't that make God responsible for my sin?

I believe I just said that God *can't* sin. Let me quote the *Westminster Confession.*

> The sinfulness thereof proceedeth only from the creature, and not from God, who, being most holy and righteous, neither is nor can be the author or approver of sin.

We do need to be doubly careful not to misunderstand. God is not and cannot be the author of sin. You and I are the authors of sin. Still, are all sinful acts under divine control? Yes. Remember our discussion of Acts 2:23 previously? God delivered Jesus up as part of His holy plan, but wicked men, after their own counsel, crucified Him. God did not sin; the *men* did. And yet, God did control their actions as part of His plan. God did not cause the wicked men to crucify Jesus. God *permitted* the wicked men to crucify Jesus. Could God have stopped the Crucifixion? Certainly, but their wicked plan was part of His righteous plan. Remember, God foreordains whatever comes to pass, even the wicked deeds of wicked men. God's own purpose overrules evil for good. Let me reiterate that God does not coerce men to sin. If He did, He would be the author of sin, which we have established is impossible and inconceivable.

> Let no one say when he is tempted, "I am tempted by God"; for God cannot be tempted by evil, nor does He Himself tempt anyone. But each one is tempted when he is drawn away by his own desires and enticed. Then, when desire has conceived, it gives birth to sin; and sin, when it is full grown, brings forth death.
> (James 1:13-15)

6. In a nutshell, are you saying that while I'm ordering a caramel latte at Starbucks, God is acting in and through me to work out His own plan?

Yes, I am. God providentially governs all aspects of existence, from the least to the greatest. You are acting, and God is acting at the same time, in and through you.

God ordains your actions, but not in a way that does violence to your will. Let me introduce one more important term:

> By the same providence, He ordereth them [all things that come to pass] to fall out, according to the nature of *second causes.*
> —*Westminster Confession,* chapter 5, section 2 (italics added)

I promised I would explain second causes. Thanks for your patience. If there are second causes, there must be first causes, right? Actually, there is only one first cause. God is, now and forever, the First Cause. God, the First Cause, then ordains whatever comes to pass through all the second causes. Have you got it? (You're supposed to say no here and ask for a better explanation or an example or both.)

Let's go back to Starbucks. You order your latte, turn to find the skim milk, trip, and spill your hot drink on a Pilates instructor who's wearing a white exercise outfit with white tights. The power you just exerted in turning and spilling your latte is real power, not an illusion.

You're a second cause in this scenario. Is the coffee also a second cause? Yes, it is. Did God, the First Cause, cause you to trip? No, in your haste, you turned too quickly, all by yourself. Did God, the First Cause, permit you to turn too quickly? Yes. Could God have intervened to keep you from turning too quickly? Yes, but His plan didn't include stopping you from turning too quickly.

What was God's purpose in that scenario? I don't know. Do you need to know? If you really needed to know, God would let you know. Sometimes we do find out what His plan was. At the end of Genesis, Joseph could see that God had always sovereignly been working out His plan. Many unbelievers had been used to bring it about:

> As for you, you meant evil against me; but God meant it for good, in order to bring it about as it is this day, to save many people alive.
> (Genesis 50:20)

Joseph finally understood all his suffering. God had a plan, and Joseph realized he had played a key part in it. I'm sure he couldn't sleep for thinking about the wisdom of God's providence. Joseph had undoubtedly passed his years in prison wondering why God had rescued him the first time. Perhaps also wondering if God had forgotten him. God did not announce His plan to Joseph. But in the end, God's plan included the rescue of Joseph's brethren, and Joseph's trials were an integral part of God's plan.

What if two years ensue and you run into the Pilates instructor at the Wednesday night prayer service? You introduce yourself and again apologize for spilling the hot latte on her white outfit. Suppose she tells you that she was so furious with you that she returned to her class ranting about the inconsiderate oaf at Starbucks. At just that moment, her landlord waltzed in and overheard her. The landlord, who is your Sunday school teacher, reminded her that a person's anger never produces the righteousness of God. Conversations ensued between the landlord and the Pilates instructor. The First Cause, God, used the second cause, the landlord, to convert the Pilates instructor. She now thanks you for turning too quickly and spilling your latte. She understands that God used it to bring about her conversion. Do you understand it now?

Most of the time we are not allowed to see God's plan so clearly. We do not need to. By faith we understand the biblical teaching that God, the First Cause, ordained whatever came to pass through a series of second causes, people and things.

> Man is not made to question, but adore.
> —Edward Young

7. Isn't it a contradiction to say that people are free and *God is sovereign?*

First of all, we are free, but we are also temporal, dependent, and fragile. God is sovereign, but he's also eternal, independent, and self-existent. As creatures, we deal with one another horizontally, but we deal with God vertically. I remind you of this so that we're clear on the limits we admit we have and the lack of limits God has.

To say that people are free and God is sovereign is not a contradiction. The essential factor is that people are free but not autonomous. To be autonomous is to be a law unto yourself. We are not a law unto ourselves. Remember, we are dependent. If we were autonomous, God could not be sovereign. To be autonomous is to be absolutely free, as God is. In fact, God is absolutely sovereign *and* absolutely autonomous.

So we need to have a concept of freedom that is remarkably short of autonomy. *We have freedom, but our freedom has limits.*

People are free enough to be held responsible for their actions, but not free enough to be autonomous. All people are responsible to the degree that they are free. God's absolute freedom limits my freedom. God's sovereignty transcends my freedom and rules over it.

Our freedom is regulated by God. He sets the boundaries. Occasionally, someone will say that my freedom limits God's sovereignty. That is patently ridiculous. If it were true, I'd be sovereign, not God.

Let me take you to the heart of this matter. If God "permits" me to sin, it does not mean that God sanctions my sin, approves of my sin, or judges it lawful. Because He does not intervene, which He could have done, and lets me sin, we are tempted to think that He is not displeased. But we would be wrong.

> Because the sentence against an evil work is not executed speedily, therefore the heart of the sons of men is fully set in them to do evil.
> (Ecclesiastes 8:11)

God's *permissive will* proves only that God has chosen to permit me to sin as I wish to. Remember, God foreordains whatever comes to pass. So, in some sense, He ordains my sin, or my sin could not happen. Why does God permit me to sin? I do not fully understand it, but this I do know: Whatever God does is holy, perfect, and infinitely wise.

6

Providential Chastening

Most Christians I meet today are dumbfounded by the notion that God chastens anyone, let alone His beloved children. Suspicious gazes and quizzical glances are ordinarily coupled with quietness following my recitation of another of our key verses:

> You have forgotten the exhortation which speaks to you as sons;
>
> "My son, do not despise the chastening of the LORD,
> Nor be discouraged when you are rebuked by Him;
> For whom the LORD loves He chastens,
> And scourges every son whom He receives."
>
> If you endure chastening, God deals with you as with sons; for what son is there who a father does not chasten? But if you are without chastening, of which all have become partakers, then you are illegitimate and not sons.
> (Hebrews 12:5-8)

This section of Scripture, in my view, is indispensable to a Christian's understanding of his or her life. At this point, you may want to go back to chapter 2 and reread my comments on these verses. Rereading that section will prepare you for our question-and-answer segment.

For Further Consideration

1. Has God promised that I'll have afflictions, and does He have a hand in them?

2. Is there a way to escape affliction altogether or at least lighten my load?

3. Can afflictions be medicinal for me?

4. Can afflictions really be necessary for me?

5. Are afflictions like tutors?

6. Do afflictions teach me things about myself I don't want to know?

7. Do afflictions conform me to Christ's image?

***

1. Has God promised that I'll have afflictions, and does He have a hand in them?

The text clearly teaches that all Christians will have afflictions, chastenings, in this life. God is sovereign. He is King. But I'm thankful that He is also Father. Father, that is, to all Christians. One must be born-again to call Him Father. The Bible does not teach that God is Father to all men but only to Christians. What, then, about unbelievers? God does have a relationship with unbelievers—He is their Creator, King, and Judge.

God not only promises all believers that they will have afflictions; He also promises that His hand will be in those afflictions. But God's hand is also in the afflictions of unbelievers. *Typically, unbelievers think God has nothing to do with them, and believers think God would never do anything to them that was painful. Both are wrong.*

The Scriptures are rife with proofs that God afflicts His children, but David makes it very clear in Psalm 119:

> I know, O LORD, that Your judgments are right,
>   And that in faithfulness You have afflicted me.
> (Psalm 119:75)

That God my Father has control over the afflictions and trials of my life should have a calming effect on me. Often it does. However, the majority of time I react as I would have before my conversion—I panic.

My wife and I laugh that I am prone, initially, to "tremble at the falling of every leaf":

> Oh Lord, when a leaf falls
> I fear you've jilted me.
> My distrust is my shame,
> And doubt my malady.
>
> I tremble at the sound
> Of a mosquito's roar
> And weary myself with
> Dark phantoms at the door.
>
> Danger disquiets me,

And my eye seeks safety
In the torturous maze
Of proud humanity.

The stars are yet secure;
Venus glides silently,
Submissively toward
Boundless eternity.

The cygnet's song echoes
Along the ridge, unheard
By a deaf creation;
The silence undisturbed.

Venus, take no thought for
Your future, and cygnet,
Be assured your pained voice
Is heard and beloved yet.

Father, forgive the vain
Fastening of my eyes
Upon the fortresses
Urged by the worldly-wise.
—W. D. Moore

I cannot imagine a fuller present reward than complete rest from all anxiety and calm confidence in a Providence which can never fail.
—C. H. Spurgeon

Only meditation on passages like Psalm 119:75 quiets me. After all these years it ought to be different, but I'm sad to say it isn't. I thank God for His patience and a fine, godly wife. How is it with you? Do you receive bad news with equanimity and understanding, remembering that God is in control, or are you more like me? Do you recognize God's fingerprints on all your troubles? Do you count on God to keep His promise to chasten you? Consider the case of history's most famous sufferer. God's sovereignty over Job's life was clear:

> The LORD gave, and the LORD has taken away;
> Blessed be the name of the LORD.
> (Job 1:21)

Job does not say the devil took away. He says the Lord took away. Even the devil needs permission to assault me. He does only what God permits. *Every creature, including Satan, is a hoe in the hand of the Almighty to turn over the soil of my life.* When an affliction comes to me, no matter who brings it, it is the Lord who sends it. He either initiates it or permits it. Either way, I'm thankful to say, it all works for my soul's good.

> Afflictions are but the shadows of God's wings.
> —George Macdonald

2. Is there a way to escape affliction altogether or at least lighten my load?

This world is a briar patch, so afflictions find everyone. They should cause us, as believers, to lift our eyes to the heavens as Jimmy Buffet's song says his father did, "looking for answers to questions that bothered him so."

"Was my past suffering necessary?" is a question on the hearts and lips of most Christians. The simple answer is yes. Your future suffering will also, one day, prove to have been necessary. Thankfully, all suffering, past, present, and future, comes from the hands of a loving Father. Disciples should be disciplined, shouldn't they? The Potter has a right to mold the clay as He wishes, right? God chastens his sons and daughters for their good, right?

> O blows that smite! O hurts that pierce
> This shrinking heart of mine!
> What are ye but the Master's tools
> Forming a work divine?
>
> Sculptor of souls! I lift to Thee
> Encumbered heart and hands;
> Spare not the chisel, set me free,
> However dear the bands.
> —Anonymous

In my own life, I've found that afflictions serve to sour me on this present world and focus me on heaven, my home.

> We should want to tarry here forever and say, "Lo this is my home," if it were not that an unkind world gives us alien treatment.
> —C. H. Spurgeon

We are all too apt to cling to this world of sorrows, for we can see it and touch it. Through afflictions, God takes our hearts off this world and reminds us that we are only pilgrims here.

> Suffering, though it is burden, is a useful burden, like the splints used in orthopedic treatment.
> —Søren Kierkegaard

Christians are often perplexed by the relative ease with which unbelievers sail through this life, some barely touched by troubles. Aren't unbelievers also under God's providential care? Why do the wicked prosper and the righteous suffer? This question has ruffled many a suffering saint throughout history. The lament of Psalm 73:5 has often proved true and bears repeating:

> They are not in trouble as other men,
> Nor are they plagued like other men.

Believers have always faced a strong temptation to envy the prosperity of the wicked. We must arm ourselves against this temptation with thoughts of God's goodness and wisdom. We know that God is sovereign, so the prosperity of the wicked is permitted in God's wisdom. We should never forget the end of unbelievers. Consideration of their end will keep us from envying them. Instead, we'll pity them.

> He observed that foolish wicked people have sometimes a very great share of outward prosperity. . . . Wicked people are really foolish people, and act against reason and their true interest, and yet every stander-by sees their prosperity. They seem to have the least share of the troubles and calamities of this life.
> —Matthew Henry

It does seem that, as a general rule, one may lighten his load of afflictions by remaining an unbeliever. Again, in general, allowing for exceptions, unbelievers often face not only fewer afflictions but also afflictions of lesser magnitude and duration. *So, if your sole goal is to minimize afflictions, you should strive to remain among the ranks of unbelievers, and you should steadfastly deny that life is short and death certain.* However, at death you will be consumed with terrors and realize too late your foolishness.

Light afflictions and prosperity have hardened and slain millions. Someone once retorted, "In the making of fools, prosperity has it all over adversity." A lighter load in this temporary world and earthly riches you can't take with you through death. Is that truly your heart's desire? Ruminate on that sentence a moment. How nearsighted you are. The other side of the river of death is eternity. Looming ahead is the specter of heavy afflictions of conscience and torment in an existence without end. No wonder the Bible instructs believers not to envy the prosperity of the wicked in this world.

I promise you, in heaven, when we will see things correctly, we will prize every affliction we've endured or are presently enduring. Why? Because we'll know that we couldn't have done without them. How do I know this? The all-wise and sovereign God ordained whatever trials came into our lives, and He did it for our good.

So let's quit whining about what the apostle Paul calls "our light affliction, which is but for a moment." Paul goes on to say that these light afflictions are "working for us a far more exceeding and eternal weight of glory" (2 Corinthians 4:17).

Do you still want to escape the afflictions that should be like diamonds to us? Sad to say, sometimes I still do. Let's hope you're more mature than I am.

3. Can afflictions be medicinal for me?

Of course. But I, for one, have never liked the taste of medicine. David reminds us in Psalm 119 that our Father afflicts us wisely: "It is good for me that I have been afflicted" (Psalm 119:71).

If we are truly godly, we know we can count on having afflictions, and they will be medicinal for us. *I cannot do without afflictions, and neither can you.* Afflictions remove the fever of worldliness from us. Afflictions flush the gold dust from our eyes by ensuring our earthly riches take wings so that we have a clearer view of heaven. God is acquainted with the diseases and distempers we have and prescribes the perfect medicines for them.

> Life is made up of sobs, sniffles, and smiles, with sniffles predominating.
> —O. Henry

Take a moment to recollect past chastenings. Weren't they timely? Just as you began to step into the street of pride without looking at the yellow flashing lights of Scripture, the God-sent purse snatcher of affliction absconded with your Coach bag. The contusions you suffered from your tumble to the pavement, the loss of your paycheck, and the calamity the theft of your Visa card entailed were, in hindsight, needful—dare I say "good" for you?

The tears, the soul-searching, and the "God, have you forgotten me's?" all worked to keep you from slipping away from God and back into the world. You were humbled, and this world's luster was tarnished for you.

> Adam in paradise was overcome, when Job on the dunghill was a conqueror.
> —Thomas Watson

> Adversity abases the loveliness of the world that might entice us.
> —Thomas Brooks

Your neglected prayer life became a thing of the past. You needed God's help.

> Trouble and perplexity drive us to prayer, and prayer driveth away trouble and perplexity.
> —Philipp Melanchthon

Your independence evaporated the moment you crashed to the pavement. Through the outward chaos, order was restored to your life. Your soul was safe again. Chastenings, seen in this light, are precious and necessary, aren't they? Remember, chastenings are God sent. He loves you as a Father should.

4. Can afflictions really be necessary for me?

Can God make a mistake? If the all-wise God afflicts me, I must need it. Again, David instructs us:

> Before I was afflicted I went astray,
> But now I keep your word.
> (Psalm 119:67)

Oh, the temptations of a season of prosperity. Verse 75 of the same psalm, you may remember, adds that God is faithful and wise when He afflicts us. What inspires the psalmist to say this? Verse 67 is plain: The psalmist had gone astray.

> Sin is going astray; and we are most apt to wander from God when we . . . think ourselves at home in the world. Prosperity is the unhappy occasion of such iniquity; it makes people conceited of themselves, indulgent of the flesh, forgetful of God, in love with the world, and deaf to the reproofs of the Lord.
> —Matthew Henry

Before the psalmist's affliction came his straying. The psalmist did not keep God's word, and God faithfully corrected him through affliction.

When I go astray or am in danger of going astray, God, in wisdom, afflicts me. When your review your life, you'll find the same to be true for you. Oh, what deep Fatherly love I see here.

Gold must be purified. The dross, or impurities, must be removed. God refines us by melting us in the furnace of affliction. We, like the Prodigal Son before us, come to our senses when we are greatly distressed, and then we return home to the Father.

> God's rod and God's love, they both stand together. It is no love in God to let men go on in sin, and never smite. God's greatest curse is when He afflicts not for sin.
> —Thomas Watson

5. Are afflictions like tutors?

Luther reckoned he couldn't correctly understand many of the psalms until *he* was in affliction. Learning *about* something and learning *from* something are distinctly different. Our individual afflictions make an impression not only on our minds but also on our hearts. We, like Luther, can better understand the psalmist's pain when we endure our own.

Afflictions insist that I search my heart and life to find where sin is lurking:

> Nothing can render affliction so unsupportable as the load of sin. Would you then be fitted for afflictions? Be sure to get the burden of your sins laid aside, and then what affliction so ever you may meet with will be very easy to you.
> —John Bunyan

I often coddle my pet sins until the rod hits my back; then I'm willing to acknowledge the vileness of my sin that God abhors. I have a tutor.

> O Lord, do not rebuke me in Your wrath,
>   Nor chasten me in your hot displeasure!
> For your arrows pierce me deeply,
>   And Your hand presses me down.
> (Psalm 38:1-2)

> There is no soundness in my flesh
>   Because of Your anger,
>   Nor any health in my bones
>   Because of my sin.
> For my iniquities have gone over my head;

> Like a heavy burden, they are too heavy for me.
> My wounds are foul and festering
> > Because of my foolishness.
>
> (Psalm 38:3-5)

> I am ready to fall,
> > And my sorrow is continually before me.
>
> For I will declare my iniquity;
> > I will be in anguish over my sin.
>
> (Psalm 38:17-18)

If I will be in anguish over my sin, God will not need to put me into anguish that I might see my sin.

Over and over in the book of Judges the people's sins cause God to raise up foreign armies to enslave or otherwise make the Israelites suffer. The suffering was their tutor, their instructor, to bring them to their senses. Their tutor taught them well, and they would retreat and return to serving and pleasing God. Of course, once the tutor departed, their sinfulness and foolishness returned.

> They provoked the LORD to anger. . . . And the anger of the LORD was hot. . . . So He delivered them into the hands of plunderers who despoiled them. . . . Wherever they went out, the hand of the LORD was against them for calamity.
> (Judges 2:12-15)

The afflictions the Lord brought taught the Israelites the wickedness of sin so they could learn to do right. Someone once quipped that those who expect to sin must expect profoundly to suffer.

My life follows the regrettable pattern established in Judges, and I have the scars to prove that afflictions, sent by a loving Father, have been my tutors. My afflictions have been faithful teachers dispatched by a loving God. When I've gone astray, they've brought me to my senses.

What of your life? Does a review of your life demonstrate that your afflictions have been your tutors? Can you now see that God employs all your troubles to refine you? If you're a born-again son or daughter of God, it is absolutely true.

> What if we have more of the rough file, if we have less rust.
> —Thomas Watson

6. Do afflictions often teach me things about myself I don't want to know?

An old proverb states that adversity has slain its thousands and prosperity its tens of thousands. I have learned that I don't handle God-given prosperity well. Earthly prosperity has normally encouraged me to be *more* earthly-minded, not less earthly-minded. That's something I've learned about myself that I'd prefer were not true. *God's blessing ought to have increased my thanksgiving, but His blessing has, instead, generally tended to confirm my pride and heighten my sense of self-reliance.* How have you done handling prosperity? Better than I have, I hope.

Afflictions, on the other hand, have humbled me and driven me closer to God. Remember our discussion on good news and bad news? At first blush, prosperity appears to be "good news." If handled improperly, prosperity proves to be "bad news." Adversity, conversely, always appears to be "bad news." However, if adversity humbles us and drives us to God, it proves to be "good news." Permit me to emphasize that we must weigh "all things" in the eternal scale. What's best for us is what's best for our souls. Adversity, more often than not, proves to be more helpful to our souls than prosperity. We are often slow to learn even the elementary things about ourselves, don't you think?

> Life without struggle and difficulty is thin and tasteless. How can a noble life be constructed if there be no difficulty to overcome, no suffering to bear?
> —C. H. Spurgeon

> Sir Fox: Corruptions of the heart masked by prosperity,
> Or Depravities in me unmasked by adversity:
> How can I judge which is the better friend to me?
> Sir Owl: Which will you give thanks for throughout eternity?
> —W. D. Moore

Perhaps we should renew our efforts to renew our minds.

> Their heart is divided;
> Now they are held guilty.
> (Hosea 10:2)

Divided loyalties call forth judgments and afflictions. When I divide my affections between God and this present world, God takes the things of this present world away from me. Is this the story of your life too?

God's judgments set people on a course of self-examination. Self-examination then uncovers a heart attempting to camouflage its love of sin and this present world. We do not like to learn the things self-examination exposes, at least I never do. But *I need them to be smoked out. How else will I slit their throats?*

> Do not lay up for yourselves treasures on earth, where moth and rust destroy and where thieves break in and steal; lay up for yourselves treasures in Heaven, where neither moth nor rust destroys and where thieves do not break in and steal. For where your treasure is, there your heart will be also. (Matthew 6:19-21)

My love for my wife cannot be divided and shared with another woman. Neither can my heart and love be divided between God and the things of the earth without God sending afflictions to correct me.

Jonah was asleep in the ship, but at prayer in the whale's belly.
—Thomas Watson

Man proposes, but God disposes.
—Thomas à Kempis

We are not at our best
Perched at the summit;
We are climbers,
At our best when the way is steep.
—John W. Gardner

God holds us over the fire of affliction to make us more straight and upright. Oh, how good it is, when sin has bent the soul away from God that affliction should straighten it again!
—Thomas Watson

7. Do afflictions conform me to Christ's image?

To begin our discussion of this question, it makes sense, I believe, to look first at the way our Lord was treated when he walked the earth:

> He was despised and rejected by men,
> A man of sorrows and acquainted with grief. . . .
> Yet we esteemed Him stricken,
> Smitten by God, and afflicted.
> But He was wounded for our transgressions.
> (Isaiah 53:3-5)

> A man of sorrows was my Lord, a sufferer, and should I expect to be exempted from suffering? He was afflicted for me and should I expect to escape affliction?
>
> Was His head crowned with thorns, and do we think to be crowned with roses?
> —Thomas Watson

I must, of course, note that Christ's sufferings were to pay for or to make satisfaction for sin, while my sufferings are chastisements and trials meant to teach me and mold me. Carrying my cross, being despised by peers, being rejected by family, and living a life of self-denial—are these not afflictions? Don't they make me more like Him? Isn't that what I want?

Again, one of our foundational Scripture texts is Romans 8:28, which, we've already seen, teaches that God works "all things" together for good for believers. It is followed by these words:

> Whom He foreknew, He also predestined to be conformed to the image of His son, that He might be the first born of many brethren.
> (Romans 8:29)

Being conformed to the image of God's son is marvelous to contemplate. What's in view here is holiness. We are to be conformed to, or brought into harmony with Christ, to walk as He walked and bear our sufferings patiently, as He bore His.

Those are deep waters. Did God know me from all eternity and decide that he would conform me to Christ? Absolutely. Can I conform myself to Christ's image? Absolutely not. My giving myself to Christ arises from the Father's giving Christ to me and me to Him. Do not shy away from this truth—revel in it! God's grace in conforming me to Christ's image will keep me safely from being conformed to this world. That path, the one chosen for me, is fraught with twists, turns, and thorns. Yet though chastened by each twist, turn, and thorn, I am certain that God will make all of them work together for my good and will use them to *conform me to Christ's image.*

> Work out your own salvation with fear and trembling; for it is God who works in you both to will and to do for His good pleasure.
> (Philippians 2: 12-13)

God whispers in our pleasures,
Speaks in our conscience,
But shouts in our pains:
It is His megaphone to rouse a dead world.
—C. S. Lewis

7

Bill, I Still Want to Avoid Chastening

Are you saying that, even after I've pointed out to you that God chastens you in love? Even after you've learned that chastenings are for your betterment? Believe me, I understand. The truth is, I'm as reluctant as you are to heartily embrace the idea that chastening is good for me, because it is just so painful.

It's apparent that you and I both prefer earthly comfort over spiritual growth. So I'll drive our need for afflictions home to both of us a little more forcefully by considering another set of questions.

For Further Consideration

1. What if afflictions will loosen our hold on this world and prepare us for the next?

2. What if afflictions are destructive to our sins?

3. What if afflictions will make us happy?

4. What if our afflictions will silence God's enemies?

***

I hope that you are finding these questions helpful in considering God's providence in your own life. I need to be reminded of these truths regularly. So let's get started.

1. What if afflictions will loosen our hold on this world and prepare us for the next?

> Our light affliction, which is but for a moment, is working for us a far more exceeding and eternal weight of glory, while we do not look at the things which are seen, but at the things which are not seen. For the things which are seen are temporary, but the things which are not seen are eternal.
> (2 Corinthians 4:17-18)

Afflictions, or chastenings, don't earn us glory, but they do prepare us for glory. Afflictions make it easier for us to focus on the unseen world, the eternal world we were created for. Without afflictions it is difficult for us to take our hearts off this visible, temporary world and its treasures and pleasures. This world's comforts, though good in themselves, can become so important to us that God must relieve us of them. Have we no time for God because our businesses beckon both day and night?

> That man is doubtless upon the brink of ruin whose earthly business eats up all his thoughts of God, of Christ, of Heaven, of Eternity, and of his soul; who can find time for anything, but none to meet with God in his closet.
> —Thomas Brooks

Has our God-given success freed up leisure time, and have we given ourselves and our time to ease and pleasure only? Do we love men's applause, which really is as light and fleeting as a June breeze?

If so, then in love, God will chasten us, send us afflictions, to remind us that riches have wings. Ease is an idol for Christians, who should remember that life is short, that pleasure of the earthly variety is not satisfactory for their souls, and that the world's applause will tomorrow be derision.

> Farewell? a long farewell to all my greatness!
> This is the state of man: today he puts forth
> The tender leaves of hopes; tomorrow blossoms,
> And bears his blushing honors thick upon him;
> The third day comes a frost, a killing frost;
> And when he thinks, good easy man, full surely
> His greatness is a-ripening, nips his root,
> And then he falls as I do.

—Cardinal Wolsey, in William Shakespeare's *Henry VIII*

Often at the pub or Starbucks I'll speak with folks about my need to rethink my philosophy of life. Wrestling with the proper way to handle money and this world's goods is a daily contest for me. I've learned not to trust them or make them my "best things," but I find it difficult to lead a balanced life. I either spend too much time tending my "things," or I have an utter disregard for them. Neither appears correct; thus, the daily wrestling match. Folks are generally willing to nod, either knowingly or condescendingly, but they all nod. Once I introduce the idea by Matthew Henry that if money were rightly estimated, "it would be feared rather than sought," the nodding ceases. Stoic old men, flashy Pilates-class devotees, and twenty-something servers all look perplexed.

I'm sympathetic, as some ideas are too preposterous to consider. That the moon is actually made of cheese would be an easier sale. I try to explain gently that money, the pursuit of it, that is, has swallowed up most of my waking hours, and I'm mostly convinced I should just simplify my life by putting the pursuit of money in its rightful place. They move from perplexed to quizzical and prepare for the punch line. When they realize I'm actually reconsidering the position of money in my life, they normally don't say much; they just do their best to keep the conversation up. It's difficult, as they never can bring themselves to "amen" what I've said. It probably ruins their day.

What about you? Do you give the devotion you owe God to the pursuit of money and career instead? Do you really want to do this? *Has devotion to the pursuit of money proven to be a worthwhile pursuit thus far?* If you gather it well, it weighs you down. Chains of gold can hold you down as effectively as iron chains can. The Bible's right when it says that if you love silver, you're never satisfied with your stash; you always want more. The happiness you seek remains elusive. It always will. Thoreau once wrote that it's bad to have a Southern slave master, worse to have a Northern one, and worst of all — to be your own slave master. Is he right? Is Thomas Brooks right? Are you on the brink of ruin, your earthly endeavors eating up your thoughts and time?

> Money has never made a man happy, nor will it. The more a man has, the more he wants. Instead of filling a vacuum, it makes one.
> —Ben Franklin

We should be thankful that God chastens us by taking away our beloved money, or at least by frustrating us in the pursuit of it when it becomes too precious to us. Losing all your money always loosens your hold on this world and its hold on you. Providence, the chastening variety, is wonderful even when it's painful, isn't it? I'm testifying from personal experience. What about you? God weans us from our love of this world by afflictions. We're glad he does, right?

2. What if afflictions are destructive to our sins?

The heat of fire is needed to remove impurities from gold. Likewise, the heat of fever is a sign that our body is fighting infection. In the same way, the heat of affliction cures pride, greed, and lust for me. Just as a fever signals to me that something is amiss in my body, affliction signals to me that God, the great Physician, is treating a disease within me.

You might say that great affliction in my life can be viewed as a regimen of spiritual chemotherapy. Strong medicines are required to remove deep-rooted and pervasive sins. I thank God that He knows precisely what my diseases are and what drug cocktail will cure them.

Sins are like termites: Both are destructive to foundations, and both love the cover of darkness. I have known homes left untreated that have literally collapsed from the damage done by termites. Who would have guessed that such tiny creatures, noiseless as they are, could fell such grand structures?

Sins do the same in my life. They silently eat away at the foundations of my life and true loves. Left untreated, sins have brought about the ruin and collapse of lofty lives, as well as lives like mine.

> One reason sin flourishes is that it is treated like a cream puff instead of a rattlesnake.
> —Billy Sunday

Afflictions stir me to action as certainly as prosperity and ease put me to rest. During periods of rest I am content with "small" sins in my life. During periods of affliction, I hunt these sins down to destroy them, fearing that they may be the cause of my chastening or a hindrance to prayer and the deliverance I seek.

> Many a ship has stood the tempest, and then has gone down in the harbour because its timbers have been gnawed to pieces by white ants. And many a man can do what is wanted in the trying

moments, and yet make shipwreck of his faith in uneventful times.
—Alexander Maclaren

Pretend you are walking into the Jefferson Street Bar and Grille. You see yourself seated on the last stool at the bar staring at CNN while Johnny Mathis purrs from the jukebox. You sidle up and sit next to yourself. Over a couple of beers you strike up a conversation. It turns out you are speaking with you as you will be precisely one year in the future. You find out that within six months you will lose your business and your home. As the future "you" details what has transpired in your life, you note that the future you does not seem shaken by all your losses.

While you commiserate with yourself, you inquire about your wife and children. The future you smiles one of those smiles that spreads slowly but certainly until it fills your face.

"The wife and children have never been happier. I don't know; the troubles just kinda brought us together. Turns out they never did care about all the "things" I cared about. I lost confidence in me, but they never did."
"Sounds like a terrific family."

"Listen, I don't know you, but you seem like a nice guy. Can I tell you something?"

You steel yourself for some bad news. "Sure."

"I was humiliated when I lost the business. Losing the house was worse, as all the neighbors were aware of my failure. I stayed in my study our last night in the house and began reading the Psalms. When I read Psalm 51, I just stopped.

127

David acknowledged his sin and said it was always before him. Are you familiar with that psalm?"

"No, I'm not."

"Well, neither was I. But it hit me. It just hit me. Not only were my sins evident to God, they were also evident to me. Does that sound just too odd for you?"

"No, go ahead. I'm more interested than you think."

"Okay. Well, my pride, my lusts, my greed, my selfishness flooded into my mind. Minutes, maybe hours, went by, I don't know. But one thing I do know — I was different."

"Wow, I don't know what to say."

"Listen, the best thing that's ever happened to me was losing my business. If that sounds crazy, I don't care. I thank God that He allowed me to lose the business. I'm focused now on my soul's interest and what's really best for my family."

"I've been reading a book that says God not only allowed you to lose your business and home, but He had a hand in it."

"Really? I need to think about that a minute. But I gotta go pick up my bride. Nice talking to you. Sorry, but I never did get your name."

"It's not important. I gotta go too. Got some reading to do — and some thinking."

Wherever you are, whoever you are, go to your own Jefferson Street Bar and Grille, no matter its name, and visualize yourself seated on that bar stool. Will the "you" of one year from now have a similar tale to tell? Will God, in love, have chastened the future you to destroy your sins? If so, why not turn to Psalm 51, repent of your sins like David, and thank God that the very knowledge that He would chasten you has brought you to your senses?

Must good times, successful times, prove to be the enemies of your soul? Must God chasten you? Will only affliction suit you as an instructor? Success, good health, and so many other things are blessings from God. Don't make Him take them from you for your soul's good.

Afflictions are destructive to our sins, and it is gracious of our Father to send afflictions to destroy what would otherwise destroy us.

3. What if afflictions will make us happy?

> Behold, happy is the man whom God corrects;
> Therefore, do not despise the chastening of the Almighty.
> For He bruises, but He binds up;
> He wounds, but His hands make whole.
> (Job 5:17-18)

We all have an aversion to suffering and pain. Christians must conquer this aversion. When we feel the sting of affliction on our backs, we must focus on our need of it. *What?* Yes, our *need* of it. Can the Almighty be wrong? Can the Eternal have judged our need improperly? It is prescribed for our good.

> Call it a chastening, which comes from the Father's love and is designed for the child's good. Call it the chastening of the Almighty, with whom it is madness to contend.
> —Matthew Henry

If we could really grasp it, we would see that God shows His affection for us in afflicting us. The angels must marvel. May I venture one step further? We should *revere* God's chastening hand. We should analyze our afflictions. What is God changing in us? What is He eradicating? I know this: We will revere all of our afflictions once we are in heaven. Will we be wise enough to revere those same afflictions, by faith, now? We should not esteem lightly evidences that we are sons or daughters of God.

> O, thou great being! What thou art
> Surpasses me to know;
> Yet sure I am, that known to Thee
> Are all Thy works below.
>
> Thy creature here before Thee stands,
> All wretched and distrest:
> Yet sure those ills that wring my soul
> Obey Thy high behest.
>
> Sure Thou, Almighty, canst not act
> From cruelty or wrath!
> O, free my weary eyes from tears,
> Or close them fast in death!
>
> But if I must afflicted be,
> To suit some wise design:
> Then man my soul with firm resolve
> To bear and not repine!
> —Robert Burns, under pressure of violent anguish

The disciplinary nature of human suffering is seldom broached in Christian circles today. How far we have veered from the tried-and-true paths of pilgrims. Pilgrims are on their way home. While they are abroad in this strange land, they draw near to God in prayers, study of the Bible, fellowship with other citizens of heaven living in this world, and in afflictions. Afflictions bring us to our Bibles and our knees. They bring us closer to God. *It is God's presence in heaven and here in this foreign land that is our soul's happiness.*

> In Your presence is fullness of joy;
> At Your right hand are pleasures forevermore.
> (Psalm 16:11)

The flute of mercy does not catch our ears as easily as the tympani of affliction does. The tympani reverberates inside us and draws us near to God. When we are in want, as the Prodigal Son was, we come to our senses and return to God and our happiness:

> He began to be in want. . . . When he came to himself, he said, ". . . I will arise and go to my father."
> (Luke 15:14-18)

His afflictions resulted in his happiness. It will prove true for us also.

4. What if our afflictions will silence God's enemies?

Critics have, at various times, charged that I serve God only from self-interest. Unfortunately, at times in my life, this indictment has been all too true. Therefore, God had me endure afflictions so that I might be changed, the charges rendered untrue, and the critics' mouths silenced.

Throughout history, it has been much the same. The devil, in particular, protested that Job served God for earthly riches:

> Have You not made a hedge around him, around his household, and around all that he has on every side? You have blessed the work of his hands, and his possessions have increased in the land. But now, stretch our Your hand and touch all that he has, and he will surely curse You to Your face!
> (Job 1:10-11)

Job's love of God was vindicated by his patient endurance of multiple, grievous afflictions. The enemy of God was silenced.

> My brethren, take the prophets, who spoke in the name of the Lord, as an example of suffering and patience. Indeed we count them blessed who endure. You have heard of the perseverance of Job and seen the end intended by the Lord—that the Lord is very compassionate and merciful.
> (James 5:10-11)

"The end intended by the Lord." That is pregnant with meaning. This I do know of Job's pains: They worked together for Job's good, for God's glory, and for the silencing of God's enemies.

Final Thoughts on Chastening

The loss of wealth often slays the pride that governs lives. It has certainly been true in my life. I may have a tendency to dwell on this aspect of chastening as it is personal to me, as your afflictions are personal to you. Your affliction may be physical suffering, mental anguish, the loss of a job, the loss of a son or daughter, or the loss of a spouse. *Afflictions, though varied, are locusts under God's control.* They are sent or permitted by God to devour our crops that we might produce a better crop. Though painful, afflictions are for our benefit:

> No chastening seems to be joyful for the present, but painful; nevertheless, afterward it yields the peaceable fruit of righteousness to those who have been trained by it.
> (Hebrews 12:11)

> Iron until it be thoroughly heated is incapable to be wrought; so God sees good to cast some men into the furnace of affliction, and then beats them on His anvil into what frame He pleases.
> —Anne Bradstreet

We are regularly tempted in times of trouble to question the goodness of God. This is insanity. Does the creature dare judge the Creator? We may banish from our poor minds all such evil thoughts. God is always perfectly wise and good.

> God whispers in our pleasures,
> Speaks in our conscience,

But shouts in our pains:
It is His megaphone to rouse a dead world.
—C. S. Lewis

"My thoughts are not your thoughts,
Nor are your ways My ways," says the LORD.
"For as the heavens are higher than the earth,
So are My ways higher than your ways,
And My thoughts than your thoughts.
(Isaiah 55: 8-9)

God's love for believers issues forth in chastenings for His beloved sons and daughters. God is pure goodness.

> Yet, in the maddening maze of things,
> And tossed by storm and flood,
> To one fixed trust my spirit clings;
> I know that God is good!
> —John Greenleaf Whittier

It is essential for you to remember that all Christians will be chastened. We have God's promise. If you are not or never have experienced chastening, you may not be a Christian. Although you are a professor in the church, you may not be a family member.

> There is no man so near the edge, so near the flames, so near hell, as he whom God will not so much as spend a rod upon.
> —Thomas Brooks

> God had one son without corruption, but no son without correction.
> —Thomas Brooks

Perhaps you can scan your memory bank and recognize times when you were being chastened but didn't recognize it for what it was. This, again, was my story. I had no idea that God was sovereign, and the concept of chastening would have been incongruous to me during the first period of my Christian life. The little I knew of the Bible was out of context, and in truth, I was a poor Bible student. I'm thankful God did not leave me in that position. Providence guided me to sound, historical Christian thinking, which, in turn, led me to a comprehension of God's sovereignty, including the blessedness of His chastening. Is God guiding you in the same direction? Thank Him for it now if He is. Your view of your life and the world will never be the same.

Aside from the affliction of riches lost, chastening in my life—and perhaps in yours—has come primarily in the form of false accusations. This is a common malady, one which I will take a moment to touch on in closing this section. *God utilizes the ruination of our reputations to reveal to us the deceitfulness of the world's applause, for which most of us have lived.* Let me paraphrase Alexander Pope. Fame and reputation are carried on the breaths of dying men. They are things difficult to maintain even while you're living. Men's applause is too fickle to be sought.

If one doesn't see the chastening hand of God in this, one can feel the pain but not be comforted during the trial.

What, you ask, is to be gained by being the victim of false accusations? First, friends immediately prove they were never really friends. By that I mean that the crowd that applauded my every move quickly became the crowd that turned on me. Have you experienced this? Did you gain a better understanding of the fickleness and unreliability of humankind? Did you gain an appreciation of God's steadfastness in times of trouble?

Were you humbled? Humility is little prized but greatly needed. These days in the church, only God seems to prize it highly. It has become evident to me that afflictions promote humility in me more than my achievements or triumphs ever could.

I could continue in a like vein, but let me end by saying that not only will afflictions help you and me *in* this life, but they will help us *through* this life, which is of greater importance.

In the treasury of great Christian hymns there is one that always comes to my mind first when discussing God's sovereignty and afflictions. Permit me to introduce you to Horatio Spafford, if you haven't met him, and a few lines from a beloved hymn he penned in 1873.

> When peace, like a river, attendeth my way,
> When sorrows like sea billows roll;
> Whatever my lot, Thou has taught me to say,
> It is well, it is well, with my soul.
>
> It is well, with my soul,
> It is well, with my soul,
> It is well, it is well, with my soul.

> Though Satan should buffet, though trials should come,
> Let this blest assurance control,
> That Christ has regarded my helpless estate,
> And hath shed His own blood for my soul.

The refrain is repeated after each stanza, and the hymn continues. Let me give you the circumstances that prompted the writing of the song.

The Chicago fire of 1871 wrecked many lives, and Mr. Spafford's was one of the fire's casualties. He was ruined financially (he had been a wealthy land investor and successful attorney). Shortly after the fire, Spafford's wife, Anna, and the couple's four daughters booked an Atlantic crossing aboard the S.S. *Ville du Havre*. There was a collision with another ship, and all four daughters perished. Anna alone survived and sent her husband a telegram that said simply, "Saved alone. What shall I do?" Tradition has it that several weeks later, as Spafford's own ship passed near the spot where his daughters had died, the Spirit inspired Horatio to pen the words above.

Afflictions of this type are tragic for unbelievers. For believers, like Horatio, afflictions of this type are indescribably painful, but not tragic. God comforted Horatio, as the hymn testifies. In addition, Horatio, as well as you and I, had God's promise that all things work together for good for believers.

DEATH OF AHAB
And a certain man drew a bow at a venture, and smote the king of Israel between the joints of the harness: wherefore he said unto the driver of his chariot, Turn thine hand, and carry me out of the host; for I am wounded ... (I Kings 22: 34)

8

A Few Questions about 1 Kings 22:34

> A certain man drew a bow at random and struck the king of Israel between the joints of his armor. So he said to the driver of the chariot, "Turn around and take me out of the battle, for I am wounded."

This is one of the foundational Scripture texts on which this little book is based. I chose it to stress the Bible's teaching that there are no "chance" events. *Fate is a fallacy.* Our God is sovereign. He upholds, directs, disposes, and governs all actions, from the greatest to the least, as the *Westminster Confession* maintains. God does this most easily and wisely. We covered the background of 1 Kings in chapter 2, in the section on our three foundational Scripture texts. If you feel you need to refresh your memory on this passage, now would be a good time to do it.

My goal, as I've repeated throughout, is that you and I apply the biblical truths we learn to our lives. With that in mind, allow me to ask a few questions about the drama in 1 Kings. Please follow my thinking, all the while applying the truths you find to your own life's drama. Remember, God is governing your life exactly as He did Ahab's.

For Further Consideration

1. Did Ahab become king without God's permission?

2. Elijah had prophesied that dogs would lick up Ahab's and Jezebel's blood. Did God govern the dogs as well as those two rank unbelievers, Ahab and Jezebel?

3. Were the four hundred false prophets employed by Ahab also governed by God?

4. Ahab plotted to ensure his own safety by exposing Jehoshaphat, the good king of Judah, to danger. Could God have stopped that plot?

5. Can anyone, including Ahab, hide from God?

6. Did the Syrian soldier who shot the arrow that wounded Ahab realize he was being used by God?

7. Did God really direct the unaimed or misaimed arrow directly to the one spot where Ahab's armor wouldn't deflect it?

My aim in this section is to focus us on God's sovereignty, but I have another goal in mind also. I want us to realize that God's sovereignty is a subject fit for tailors, bartenders, accountants, and pimps, as well as a Sunday school class. What I mean is this. As I listen to Christians talk about witnessing, I can see that "witnessing" has become as narrow and one-dimensional as ever could be imagined. I attribute this to the modern emphasis on "decisionalism." Much of Christianity, sadly, has been reduced to a "do you accept Jesus" mentality. Instead of admiring a rose bush in full bloom, we're focused on a nodule that's about to break through the stem just before the last April snow. Folks, it's time we restore a Christian understanding to the church and the world.

Is God sovereign over the pimp's life? Over the accountant's life? Over the tailor's life? Is God sovereign over the salvation of the tailor, bartender, and pimp?

Is God sovereign over the life and salvation of every member of the Sunday school class? Then let's storm the church and the world with fresh vigor, believing that our shilly-shallying misrepresents and dishonors our sovereign God.

Only souls matter. The world is full of them, and the church has a few. Can't we discuss life with them? Are we capable of discussing life with them? *Every discussion of life includes a discussion of God's sovereignty, doesn't it? How else can a bartender make sense of her broken leg?* God is sovereign over every one of His enemies, right? Then let's go talk about life with them. Christ will enter as the answer somewhere in the discussion. I promise.

If your Christian witness is limited to one of the short, popular evangelism tools such as the bridge illustration or others, you need to rethink what you term "witnessing." We are not of the world, but we are in it. Let's decide to take our witness to it. Go to the barbershop, bank, and pub with a determination to integrate God's sovereignty into a discussion of the *lives* of the people you meet there. They are the focus, not you. Listen to their heartaches and triumphs and ask questions that will lead to a pondering of

God's place and power in the events of their lives. You'll be surprised how the sovereign God will bless your efforts. Sovereignty gives significance to lives, which is what every one of us craves. Most of us are just looking for it in the wrong places. Now, on to the questions.

***

1. Did Ahab become king without God's permission?

> Ahab, risen to the throne?
> Cruelty adorns his crown.
> Murderer glittering as
> He struts, mortal of renown.
>
> Does the Almighty not see?
> Does God not care, or is He
> Unable to discharge this
> Champion of infamy?
> —W. D. Moore

This question is at the heart of any discussion of God's sovereignty. Just how far does it extend?

Ahab couldn't have become king without at least two things happening for certain. Number one, Ahab must have desired it and taken action to bring it to pass. Number two, God must have permitted it. God gave Ahab breath every night when he was asleep, right? God is sovereign over the day of death, right? God could have called for Ahab's breath to cease, ending his life at any moment, right? Since He didn't, God must have decided, wisely, that evil Ahab should be king. Again, we see the free will of man alongside the sovereign rule of God.

2. *Elijah had prophesied that dogs would lick up Ahab's and Jezebel's blood. Did God govern the dogs as well as those two rank unbelievers, Ahab and Jezebel?*

Lest you protest that I'm being harsh with Ahab and Jezebel, please accept this testimony from the Scriptures:

> There was no one like Ahab who sold himself to do wickedness in the sight of the LORD, because Jezebel his wife stirred him up.
> (I Kings 21:25)

Enough said about their character. If there's one category you don't want to be the best in, it's "best at doing wickedness in the sight of the Lord."

If God could not govern the dogs, how could He be sure they'd be nearby when needed?

> Now when Jehu had come to Jezreel, Jezebel heard of it; and she put paint on her eyes and adorned her head. . . . Then, as Jehu entered at the gate, she said, "Is it peace, Zimri, murderer of your master?" . . .
> Two or three eunuchs looked out at [Jehu]. Then he said, "Throw her down." So they threw her down and some of her blood spattered on the wall and on the horses. . . . So they went to bury her, but they found no more of her than the skull and the feet and the

> palms of her hands. . . . And he said, This is the word of the LORD . . . saying, "On the plot of ground at Jezreel dogs shall eat the flesh of Jezebel."
> (2 Kings 9:30-36)

> [Ahab] died and was brought to Samaria. . . . Then someone washed the chariot at a pool in Samaria, and the dogs licked up his blood while the harlots bathed, according to the word of the LORD which He had spoken.
> (I Kings 22:37-38)

The sovereignty of God is as awe inspiring as it is far reaching. The dogs completed Jezebel's and Ahab's ruin and shame. Did the dogs appear because they wanted to? Yes. Did the dogs lick up the royal blood because they liked it naturally? Yes. Is God governing the dogs as well as the dogs' natures? Yes.

Jezebel easily excelled her miserable husband in wickedness, treachery, and pride. Therefore, God ordered greater shame in her case. Nothing was left of her but her skull (the painted face was gone), her feet, and her hands. God's justice was delivered by God's sovereignty.

Can you and I translate this into our lives? What about the troublesome raccoons in your backyard? What of the meddlesome neighbor up the lane? Is the Almighty sovereign over the raccoons and the neighbor? Of course, He is. He's working out His story, remember? How do they, the raccoons and the meddlesome neighbor, fit into your life now that you are looking through the spectacles of sovereignty? Can God use them to prove and improve your faith? I think you know the answer.

3. Were the four hundred false prophets employed by Ahab also governed by God?

> The king of Israel gathered the prophets together, about four hundred men, and said to them, "Shall I go up against Ramoth Gilead to fight, or shall I refrain?"
> So they said, "Go up, for the Lord will deliver it into the hand of the king."
> (I Kings 22:6)

Most prophets in that age were desirous of pleasing their patrons, usually the kings, by prophesying what the kings wanted to hear. So, of course, they encouraged Ahab in the expedition and assured him of success.

The four hundred prophets prophesied falsely and flatteringly as they longed to. God certainly permitted it. He could have stopped all their mouths. Well, couldn't He have? There is something more intriguing taking place that demonstrates even better the extent of God's sovereignty. Micaiah, a true prophet of God, is summoned, and he predicts Ahab's defeat and death:

> "I saw all Israel scattered upon the hills as sheep that have not a shepherd." The purport of this was that the army of Israel would be defeated and dispersed, that Ahab would fall in the battle.
> —Jamieson, Fausset, Brown Commentary

Micaiah informs Ahab that God permitted Satan, by the prophets, to deceive him into his destruction.

> The LORD said, "Who will persuade Ahab to go up, that he may fall at Ramoth Gilead?" . . . Then a spirit came forward and stood before the LORD, and said, "I will persuade him." . . . "I will go out and be a lying spirit in the mouth of all his prophets."
> (I Kings 22: 20-22)

It was a lie, from the father of lies, but it was given by the Almighty's permission.

Lest we misunderstand, let's give an ear to Matthew Henry:

> This matter is here represented after the manner of men. We are not to imagine that God is ever put upon new counsels, or is ever at a loss for means whereby to effect His purposes, nor that He needs to consult with angels, or any creature, about the methods He should take nor that He is the author of sin or the cause of any man's either telling or believing a lie. . . . He is continually attended and served by an immeasurable company of angels . . . ready to go where He sends them and to do what He bids them, messengers of mercy on His right hand, of wrath on His left hand. That He . . . presides over all the affairs of this lower world, and overrules them according to the counsel of His own will.

Wow! God presides over the affairs of this world by various means after the counsel of His will.

> The rise and fall of princes, the issues of war, and all the great affairs of state . . . are no more above God's direction than the meanest concerns of the poorest cottage are below his notice.
> —Matthew Henry

Think of it, the lying spirits, by God's permission, deceived the false prophets. Were the false prophets aware of it? No. Were they doing God's will? Yes.

We find similar teaching in the book of Job. There, Satan, by divine permission, is allowed to torment Job. Earlier, God had put a hedge of protection around Job. Isn't it clear that all men and creatures, even wicked ones, do what they wish, but only by divine permission?

I must reiterate that history is His story. Be mindful that our God does everything in goodness, righteousness, and wisdom. If this is new to you and difficult for you to digest, believe me when I say you're not alone. The truth of it, however, is unassailable.

> It ain't those parts of the Bible that I can't understand that bother me, it is the parts that I do understand.
> —Mark Twain

4. Ahab plotted to ensure his own safety by exposing Jehoshaphat, the good king of Judah, to danger. Could God have stopped the plot?

Let me ask you, can omnipotence and omniscience bring about the desired end of all matters? Can the Almighty's infinite power and infinite knowledge be withstood? Can anyone cause a delay in God's execution of His plan?

Ahab plotted. It sounds ridiculous, doesn't it? It has long been true, as Thomas à Kempis said, that man proposes and God disposes. Ahab plotted, and by earthly standards of wisdom, the plot was ingenious. God permitted Ahab's plan to proceed. God certainly could have cut it off at any point. But the wicked plan ran its course, and to earthly eyes, it nearly worked. To heavenly eyes, all such plans are laughable.

> The wicked plots against the just,
>   And gnashes at him with his teeth.
> The Lord laughs at him,
>   For He sees that his day is coming.
> (Psalm 37:12-13)

Ahab is proud and insolent, and Ahab does not see that this day is the day of his death. His day has come. Ahab's vile plan will be vain and ineffectual.

He contested with God. He trekked to Ramoth Gilead to fight the Syrians and to deceive Jehoshaphat and God. The wicked foolishly underestimate the One against whom they war.

God is in heaven. He oversees all people and all their projects. His power easily overcomes and overrules all human attempts. God is at ease and at rest, out of the reach of impotent creatures and their follies. The children of men have a Judge in all their affairs; one secure in His ability to accomplish His plan, purpose, and design, despite the opposition of all creatures.

I sit here in wonder, considering the paragraph I've just written. *The perfect power and repose of the Eternal Mind should quell all of my fears.* Why do the plots of the wicked in my life discomfort and disquiet me? Have I, like Ahab, forgotten that God is in heaven, laughing at my enemies?

The other night, my Lois, after patiently listening to my fearful report about this or that, faxed me this, or something close to it.

> In light of God's sovereignty, it is your duty and privilege to be fearless.
> —Matthew Henry

Can you see why I adore her?

The past three and a half years have been the most trying period of my life. Wicked men have designed to ruin my life and reputation. I have not, at this moment, been assured they will not be successful. To distrust God when one understands providence is shameful. My understanding of providence must have penetrated my mind but not my heart. Only as I have been writing this little book have I found the peace I've been seeking for three and a half years. May you be wiser than I. God does rest at ease in His heavens, fully able to thwart the plans of the wicked in my life and yours.

One thing I do know: I wouldn't have drawn near to God or written this book if God had not permitted my wicked men a long leash—longer than I thought was necessary. I'm thankful that God doesn't rule by my thoughts or yours.

Consider your enemies past and present. Did God use their success with their plots to draw you near to Him? If so, then their wickedness served God and you well. We must not fret the occasional success of wicked designs against us. Their end will be their shame. Remember, God is not just watching; He is watching *over* us. God will stop their plots at just the right time, the time that perfectly fits His plan. If God permits my wicked enemies' plans to succeed, it will be because it's best. His glory and my soul's good are at stake, so He will do what's best.

Let's go one step further. What if God permits the lies of wicked men to send me to prison? Will I embrace my cell, knowing that God will make "all things," including imprisonment on false charges, work for my good and His glory? I'm persuaded—no, *convinced*—that God will strengthen me when I need to be strengthened. Would my imprisonment be just? No, but all that will get straightened out in heaven. Would my imprisonment benefit my soul? Of course. If God permits it, my soul will profit from my suffering. I have God's word on it. Life is exciting, you know?

> If our times were in our own hand, we would have deliverance, too soon; if they were in our enemy's hand, we should have deliverance too late.
> —Thomas Watson

5. Can anyone, including Ahab, hide from God?

Ahab schemed to secure himself and expose his friend Jehoshaphat.

> The king of Israel said to Jehoshaphat, "I will disguise myself and go into battle; but you put on your robes." So the king of Israel disguised himself and went into battle.
> (I Kings 22:30)

Ahab pretended to honor Jehoshaphat by making him commander of the joint armies. But Ahab really sought to hide himself from God's view. Let no one attempt to hide from God's view or judgment.

> O LORD, You have searched me and known me.
> You know my sitting down and my rising up;
>   You understand my thought afar off.
> You comprehend my path and my lying down,
>   And are acquainted with all my ways.
> (Psalm 139:1-3)

David here personalizes our answer in a prayer: "You have searched me and known me." His sincerity and reverence befit such a contemplation. All things are naked before our God. His knowledge is perfect. Both outward actions and inward thoughts lie open to our Creator.

King David's heart was on display to God. David's waking, rising, resolving, and resting were comprehended by God every moment. The same held true for Ahab.

> He is acquainted with all our ways, intimately acquainted with them; He knows what rule we walk by, what end we walk towards, what company we walk with.
> —Matthew Henry

We, like Ahab, are foolish to think we can hide from God. Ahab's disguise thwarted the Syrians, but not God.

> A certain man drew a bow at random.
> (I Kings 22:34)

Random Syrians drawing random bows shooting random arrows into the ranks of nameless Israelite soldiers. Nameless to me and nameless to the Syrians , but not nameless to God. The "random" arrow found its way between the joints of the disguised one's armor. Stunning, isn't it?

> Indeed, the darkness shall not hide from You,
> > But the night shines as the day;
> > The darkness and the light are both alike to You.
> (Psalm 139:12)

Nothing can hide Ahab from God. Nothing can hide you or me from God. God's will was accomplished. Ahab was found out and executed. None of people's "random" acts are random to God, are they?

David says in Psalm 139 that "such knowledge is too wonderful for me." I concur. Under the cover of darkness I've done things that would make wicked men blush. Perhaps the same is true of you. The darkness shielded my sin from you and your sin from me. Darkness shields nothing from God's eyes. He dwells in eternal noontime brightness. All things are visible to Him. May you and I repent in sorrow that we would ever think to hide from our Judge. The darkness and light are alike to the One who separated the light from the darkness for us. Ahab, you and I—in God's sight, at all times, to bring about His plan.

6. Did the Syrian soldier who shot the arrow that wounded Ahab realize he was being used by God?

Surely the Syrian soldier began the day in trepidation and ended it with jubilation, assuming the soldier lived out the day. From his perspective, the impending battle was probably disconcerting as war carries in its bosom the possibility of death. The soldier did not seek out service to God, nor was he rewarded by God for his timely service. Nevertheless, that soldier who drew the random bow and shot the random arrow was serving God as fully as Jehoshaphat was.

With no particular target in mind, the soldier let fly. With so many troops on the field, the probability was high that the arrow would strike someone. That it would kill someone was improbable, as these were armored soldiers. But the Syrian raised his bow, and the shaft whistled through the sky. Before Ahab's arrow found the joint in Ahab's armor, the Syrian was probably reaching for another arrow. How many "random" arrows he shot isn't recorded, but each one reached its mark. Let me repeat that. Each arrow reached its mark, the mark God aimed at.

Did all of the Syrian's other arrows strike the earth rather than the enemy? If so, were the arrows that missed any less under the providence of God? If one of the Syrian's arrows was deflected by a helmet or shield, was the deflection part of God's plan? Were all of the arrows, casualties, and victories that day part of God's plan and under God's control? Yes. Were the Syrian archer and all of the other combatants of both armies acting of their own free will? Yes.

Mystifying? Yes, and awe inspiring. Do you object that it can't be because you don't completely understand it? Should God's wisdom be stunted by your mortal limitations? *The Bible clearly teaches that the free actions of men and the sovereignty of God work hand in hand. Only our arrogance causes us to open our mouths in protest when we should be opening them in praise.*

Remember, God's will was the first cause. The Syrian and his arrow were second causes. As the *Westminster Confession* reminds us,

> All things come to pass immutably, and infallibly; yet by the same providence, He ordereth them to fall out, according to the nature of second causes.

The Creator upholds, directs, disposes, and governs all creatures, actions and things, from the greatest to the least to the praise of the glory of His wisdom, power, justice, goodness, and mercy, to borrow the language of the Confession. Oh, the riches and depths of providence.

Is your life the exception? Of course not. Your life, like the Syrian's, is governed by God, whether you sit in the last pew of Winnetka Bible Church or on the last stool at the end of the bar at Little Ricky's.

7. Did God really direct the unaimed or misaimed arrow directly to the one spot where Ahab's armor wouldn't deflect it?

> The doctrine of providence excludes both necessity and chance from the universe, substituting for them the intelligent and universal control of an infinite, omnipresent God.
>
> —Charles Hodge

Does it seem I'm retracing the same steps we took earlier? I prefer to think of it as viewing a diamond from many angles. Only then can you appreciate its color, cut, and clarity. *Resignation* to God's sovereignty, providentially worked out through the actions of people with free wills is not my goal. My goal is that you and I *revel* in God's providential workings in our lives. This understanding of God's government of *our* world enlightens and energizes us. Our lives and actions do make a difference—often *the* difference, as the Syrian's arrow demonstrated. Kings are disposed of and others elevated by men's actions under God's government. I want us to see the world differently from before. I want us to see the world differently from the way our neighbors do. I want us to see the world as Christians should! Let's take another look at that diamond.

Did Ahab stand or crouch? Was Ahab in the exact spot on the battlefield he needed to be at the precise moment he needed to be? Was that gust of wind that altered the arrow's flight rising at just the right time? Did the Syrian soldier hesitate until his comrade moved out of his way? Did the Syrian stumble as he launched his arrow, lowering its trajectory? For heaven's sake, was the Syrian born precisely when he needed to be in the country he needed to be? Did God keep him safe through other battles that he might be alive and well to fire off Ahab's arrow?

Can you see why Charles Hodge said chance was excluded? God has absolute control over circumstances. This control extends to all events.

This has repercussions for you and me. The circumstances of our births and families are under God's control, and they matter. What if you'd been born in Saginaw, Michigan? What schools would you have attended? What friends would you have made? What person would you have married? Who gave you your talents and denied you others? Are you prone to health? Who made you so? Are you sickly? Who made you so? Nothing happened or happens by chance in your life or mine. *There are no random arrows or random events in your life.* God has a purpose, and His will has been and is being done.

> The LORD kills and makes alive;
>   He brings down to the grave and brings up.
> The LORD makes poor and makes rich;
>   He brings low and lifts up.
> (I Samuel 2:6-7)

Can you see that God's will brings meaning to your life? What of your pain? *Providence gives meaning to your pain. You didn't suffer randomly as you feared.* There was purpose in it—God's purpose. Your place in history and your history are meaningful in the light of providence.

Were you abandoned by your father? Exposed to unwanted relationships with various men by your mother? Disfigured by that teen auto wreck? Victimized by your wife's adultery? Bruised by your ex-husband's slander, as well as his fists? You are not alone. Each of us has pain. But providence gives meaning to our pain. Remember Sascha? The train took her leg, but only because God permitted it. The loss of her leg was both painful and providential. May we learn to rejoice in the beauty of God's providence in our lives.

> Do not thou presume to be the governor of the world, but leave the reins of government in His hands that made it, and best knows how to rule it.
> —John Flavel

The next chapter will introduce you to a character who should be dear to all of you who have suffered at your family's hand. His name is Jephthah.

9

I Had A Rough Childhood—*So What?*

> Jephthah the Gileadite was a mighty man of valor, but he was the son of a harlot; and Gilead begot Jephthah. Gilead's wife bore sons and when his wife's sons grew up, they drove Jephthah out. . . . Then Jephthah fled from his brothers and dwelt in the land of Tob; and worthless men banded together with Jephthah, and went out raiding with him. (Judges 11:1-3)

Jephthah is best known for making an ill-advised vow that brought about the death of his daughter. But I wish to focus on his beginnings and God's purpose. If you're puzzled over your birth and upbringing, please apply the insights you gain from Jephthah's struggles to your own struggles. Jephthah was born to the right family at the right time under the seemingly wrong circumstances, but God governed it all. You, too, were born to the right family at the right time, perhaps under the seemingly wrong circumstances. God governed your birth and your circumstances as well:

> You formed my inward parts;
>   You covered me in my mother's womb. . . .
> My frame was not hidden from You,
>   When I was made in secret,
>   And skillfully wrought in the lowest parts of the earth.
> Your eyes saw my substance, being yet unformed.

> And in Your book they all were written,
> The days fashioned for me,
> When as yet there were none of them.
> (Psalm 139:13, 15-16)

God made us and knows us. Our secret tears and sighs are known to Him and are precious. David said God "covered" us in our mothers' wombs, so I doubt not He can uncover us. When we were hidden from human eyes, we were not hidden from His eyes. He governed us in the womb, and He governs us now. Yet we were all born in the ordinary course of nature. See what reasons you and I have to praise God and His providence?

I have no idea how old Jephthah was when he discovered that he was different from his brothers. Cruelty seldom keeps us in the dark for long. Gilead, Jephthah's father, had sinned with a harlot, and Jephthah was the fruit of that sinful union. *His life began in disgrace, through no fault of his own.*

> The babe that's born not of legitimate birth is considered a sort of intruder on earth.
> —Horace C. Carlisle

It was a distinct disadvantage to be an illegitimate child, a bastard. Jephthah's brothers put him out of the family without an inheritance.

> One would not have thought this abandoned youth was intended to be Israel's deliverer and judge, but God often humbles those whom he designs to exalt. . . . So Joseph, Moses, and

> David, the three most eminent of the shepherds of Israel, were all thrust out by men, before they were called of God to their great offices.
> —Matthew Henry

God intended Jephthah to deliver Israel at a future date. How does God prepare Jephthah for the task? God permits Jephthah's brothers to disinherit him and cast him out. Had Jephthah no feelings? Of course he had. But God knew best. I do not read that Jephthah's brothers were men of valor. Perhaps their prosperous upbringing had spoiled them for service. Luxury rarely begets bravery. *Rough conditions, however, often prepare a man for daring duty.*

> God's people have no writ of ease granted them, no charter of exemption from trouble in this life. While the wicked are kept in sugar, the godly are often kept in brine.
> —Thomas Watson

Verse 1 informs us that Jephthah was a man of valor. This designation he acquired while roaming the land of Tob with other "worthless" men. Perhaps "rabble" better defines this group. Over a period of years, God's hero was being molded for his particular service, but I feel certain he was unaware of it. On the contrary, Jephthah must have felt abused. His life must have been a mystery to him. But it was no mystery to God.

Consider the second causes in this drama. Gilead sinned. Did God cause it? Heaven forbid! God is not the author of sin:

> Let no one say when he is tempted, "I am tempted by God," for God cannot be tempted by evil, nor does He Himself tempt anyone. But each one is tempted when he is drawn away by his own desires and enticed.
> (James 1:13-14)

Gilead's sin, the mother's sin, and the brothers' enmity were all governed by God for His holy purpose. Simply amazing! Remember, God foreordained whatever came to pass without violating Gilead's, the mother's, or the brothers' free will. Yet the actions of these people, sinful as they were, were so under the control of God that they occurred only by His permission and in execution of His purposes.

Thinking back on all the unhappy circumstances of my boyhood makes Jephthah's story personal to me: A father who left early in my life but who, in truth, would have done me a favor if he'd left even earlier. Injuries that ended my dreams fueled my anger. These, as well as many other experiences, shaped me.

Jephthah had his land of Tob. I had mine. Mine was the Century Lounge, the Whirlaway, The Towne Lounge, and The Dew Drop Inn. Jephthah's worthless men are nameless in the Scriptures; mine were not. There was The Thin Man, Cigar John, Boston Shorty, Cornbread Red, Jake, and Dominic, to name a few. Jephthah went raiding; I went thieving. His raiding was probably righteous. My thieving certainly was not.

Eventually, God would allow Jephthah to grasp the reasons for his suffering. It was kind of God. It seems God has likewise been kind to me. I'm no Jephthah in scope of duty and service to God, but I am seeing that I was fitted by my peculiar circumstances for my own service to my Master. My background has often embarrassed me. In retrospect, it seems to have been indispensable. As I walk through this world, my eyes see things others may not. I don't mean I see better or more deeply. I mean only that I see differently. God providentially made sure I would. Sad-eyed bartenders who smile too much, bright-eyed shoeblacks who smile too little, and sixty-year-old madams with Lucky Strike tattoos all are drawn to me, and I to them. Why? God made it so. Their grandfathers, uncles, and sisters were my friends.

God shaped me—but it nearly broke my heart. God's sculpting, of course, was perfect. What about you? Can you see yourself in Jephthah's story? Do you have your own sad tale? your own heartaches? your own shame? Undoubtedly you do. Could it be that God has been preparing you, in your own land of Tob, for special service?

Does your life still look the same to you? What has God been preparing you for? How has God molded you through the pain inflicted by other human beings? Did they mean it for your good? No. But God did.

For Further Consideration

1. When did the elders of Gilead decide Jephthah should lead them? When did God decide Jephthah should lead them?

2. Judges 11:7 records this question from Jephthah to the elders of Gilead: "Did you not hate me, and expel me from my father's house?" Did they, in fact, hate Jephthah as part of God's plan?

3. Judges 11:9 quotes Jephthah again: "If you take me back home to fight against the people of Ammon, and the LORD delivers them to me, shall I be your head?" Was Jephthah right to attribute a possible victory to God?

4. Judges 11:11 continues, "Jephthah spoke all his words before the LORD in Mizpah." It seems Jephthah spread the whole affair before the Lord in prayer. But if God foreordains whatever comes to pass, why pray at all?

We have for our consideration the strange road taken by our bastard, exiled hero. Only providence can provide an answer to his life, your life, and mine.

***

1. When did the elders of Gilead decide Jephthah should lead them? When did God decide Jephthah should lead them?

Men make decisions in time. For us, events happen in an order, in a sequence, time being integral to our gathering of information.

> It came to pass after a time that the people of Ammon made war against Israel. . . . The elders of Gilead went to get Jephthah from the land of Tob. Then they said to Jephthah, "Come and be our commander."
> (Judges 11:4-6)

Our earthly existence and all it includes, including decision making, takes place in time. Notice the references above: "It came to pass after a time"; "the elders of Gilead went"; "then." War began, followed by the elders' going, followed by their making a request of Jephthah. This is ordinary life to us in this world. Time is our present realm. In the next world, we will be in eternity, and time will not be a part of it.

God has always existed in eternity, where time does not exist. God doesn't learn anything sequentially. Think of it— God has always known all things simultaneously. God doesn't learn anything, He knows all as a present reality and always has. Remember that the *Westminster Confession* said,

> By the same providence, He ordereth them to fall out, according to the nature of second causes.

Nothing is contingent with God. Let me explain. Suppose you are walking a few feet in front of me at the mall. We come to a point where you may turn either to the right or to the left. I must wait to see which way you turn so I will know which way to turn if I wish to follow you. My action is contingent upon your action. I must learn what you will do before I can act.

God already knows which way you'll turn. He doesn't wait and watch and learn. God knows already and has known from all eternity which way you'll turn at the mall. There was never a time He didn't know which way you'd turn. He knows all things like this. He's different from us, wouldn't you say?

Sometimes Christian teachers will agree that God knows which way you'll turn at the mall, but they teach that God does it by looking down the corridors of time to see which way you'll turn. They have set themselves against the Bible at this point. Can you see the problem? God would still be learning, wouldn't He? If He's still learning, then God isn't all-knowing. Without the all-knowing part (omniscience), God would cease to be God!

God knows which way you'll turn because He upholds, *directs*, disposes and governs you as well as your actions, both great and small, by His most wise and holy providence. *Whew!* The majesty of God is restored with each passing thought of His knowledge and power, isn't it?

The elders of Gilead decided *after* the trouble began that Jephthah should lead them. God decided apart from time that Jephthah should lead. God always knew Jephthah would lead because He always willed it.

You should have a migraine about right now, so let's return to this later. Does this seem to be far over your head? If so, I understand completely. I'll never forget how I felt the first time I heard these ideas. I realized quickly that I had some hard work ahead of me because as I was lagging behind in my understanding of the Bible. If you're feeling the same way, just hang in there. In the next chapter we'll meet a beautiful woman who will help us understand better how God governs His world. You're okay with learning from beautiful women, aren't you?

2. Judges 11: 7 records this question from Jephthah to the elders of Gilead: "Did you not hate me, and expel me from my father's house?" Did they, in fact, hate Jephthah as part of God's plan?

Yes, all things are a part of God's plan. Notice, I did not say their hate was a good thing. In fact, it was evil. Was Jephthah's expulsion by his brothers with the elders' agreement a part of God's plan? Yes. Was the expulsion a good thing in and of itself, a righteous thing? The expulsion may have been lawful, but it was as heartless and unloving as it appears. Therefore, it would be evil. Was it still a part of God's good plan? Yes.

This brings us back to Romans 8:28. God was making all things (good and bad things) work together for Jephthah's good. This is exactly what He does in your life and mine, if we love Him and are called according to *His purpose*.

This is another example of concurrence, which we looked at earlier. The brothers and elders meant Jephthah's expulsion for evil, but God meant it for good. In this drama, we can see the confluence of God's intention and men's intentions. Instead of overruling the brothers' and elders' desires, God *transcended* them, and by His great power brought good out of evil.

He has done and is doing exactly that for believers right now. It's fun to learn how the world actually works, isn't it? *God is no spectator. He's an orchestrator.* Before we move on, I want to stress again that evil is not good. Gilead's consorting with a harlot was evil, a sin. But God can bring good *out of* evil. Therefore, we can say that evil worked out for good, but we must not call evil good. That would be sinful.

3. Judges 11:9 quotes Jephthah again: "If you take me back home to fight against the people of Ammon, and the LORD delivers them to me, shall I be your head?" Was he right to attribute a possible victory to God?

God had taken Jephthah from obscurity and thrust him into the limelight. Jephthah was not overly confident that God would deliver the Israelites. He was aware that God was using the Ammonites to chasten Israel, and the chastening might not yet be complete. Therefore, we see the implied "if" in his question.

If Jephthah's confidence in victory was uncertain, his confidence in himself was even more uncertain. That in itself is beautiful. Independent bands of men and their leaders tend toward self-reliance. We sense none of this in Jephthah. God had thrust him into the limelight, and he would return the honor. If there was to be a victory, Jephthah would correctly attribute it to God. *Jephthah would acknowledge God's hand in the matter, whether the outcome was victory or defeat:*

> A man's heart plans his way,
> But the LORD directs his steps.
> (Proverbs 16:9)

It would still have been God's providence if Jephthah had been defeated, right? Most folks I speak with, as I mentioned earlier, can be persuaded to attribute to God and His providence the "good things" that happen in their lives, but they are hesitant to attribute to God and His providence the "bad things" that befall them. Is this true of you? Is God, in your mind, responsible only for the "good things" in your life? Surely you remember our discussion of chastening. God governs those chastening things as well. Did the cyclone that destroyed your wheat crop operate independently of God? Are the slanderous things your ex-boss said outside of God's control? Let me emphasize that God could not make "all things" work together for good for those who love Him if He were not sovereign over "all things," whether good or bad.

4. Judges 11:11 continues, "Jephthah spoke all his words before the Lord in Mizpah." It seems Jephthah spread the whole affair before the Lord in prayer. But if God foreordains whatever comes to pass, why pray at all?

Jephthah lived with his eye toward the Lord and would do nothing without consulting Him. He did not depend on his own understanding and courage; he depended on God's strength and favor. May you and I emulate this humble man's practice. What is begun prayerfully is likely to end prosperously.

The question of the necessity of prayer to an all-knowing, foreordaining God is a reasonable one. It is sometimes framed this way: Does prayer change God's mind?

Let's back up a moment. We know that God does all things with a purpose. God was working all things together for Jephthah's good, and at the same time, He was working all things together to accomplish His eternal purpose. We should focus a minute on the "how" of His workings.

God's providence extends to the means as well as to the ends. Remember our discussion of secondary causes? God wanted to deliver the Israelites, so He trained Jephthah for the task through a series of secondary causes: the sexual sin of his father, the mistreatment by his brothers, and the request of the elders for Jephthah's help. Notice that two of the examples are sinful but one is not. They are, nevertheless, the means God uses to bring about His purpose. God governs all.

Well, then, where does prayer fit in? Prayer is an acknowledgment of our dependence. We give thanks because we are dependent. We make requests for help because we are dependent. *God is not benefited by our prayers; we are.* What benefit could God receive? He doesn't need prayers to make Him happy or fulfilled. He is and has been eternally happy and fulfilled. Creating us didn't alter His happiness. He is perfect.

Does God learn from the information we give Him in prayer? That's laughable. He already knows all things.

Prayer does not change God's mind. His plan and the execution of that plan are perfect. You and I learn something today that we didn't know yesterday, and we change our minds. If we learn something relevant to our situations again today, we'll wisely change our minds again. God *never* learns anything, so He never changes His mind.

Is prayer a waste of time then?

> Is anyone among you suffering? Let him pray. Is anyone cheerful? Let him sing psalms. Is anyone among you sick? Let him call for the elders of the church, and let them pray over him, anointing him with oil in the name of the Lord. And the prayer of faith will save the sick, and the Lord will raise him up. And if he has committed sins, he will be forgiven. Confess your trespasses to one another, and pray for one another, that you may be healed. The effective, fervent prayer of a righteous man avails much. (James 5:13-16)

Why would we be encouraged to pray when someone is suffering if it were a waste of time and effort? Why would the elders pray over the sick if God were not willing to change their condition and raise them up? Why would James write of *effective*, fervent prayer that avails much if it didn't? So if prayer doesn't change God, what does it change? Prayer, first of all, changes us. When we are sick or suffering, perhaps under financial strain, for example, we cry out to God, and our dependence becomes obvious to us. A view of our dependence, frailty, and weakness changes us by humbling us. *We come to see ourselves and God more accurately in troubled times.*

Our condition in this world is constantly in a state of flux, and that is owing to God's providence. Prosperity for a season and then adversity for a season? Both come from God's hand to you. Remember,

> In the day of prosperity be joyful,
> But in the day of adversity consider:

> Surely God has appointed the one as well as the other.
> (Ecclesiastes 7:14)

Prosperity ought to birth prayers of praise. Prosperity ought to humble us as we acknowledge that it was brought by God, not by us. Normally, as you may know from your own life, prosperity becomes a rock to stumble over. We become proud, boastful, self-indulgent, and neglectful of prayer. Earlier I mentioned an old saying of which I often remind myself:

> Adversity has slain its thousands,
> Prosperity its tens of thousands.

Ingratitude causes a man to beat proudly on his breast. Personally speaking, if I will not go to my knees in gratitude, God will drive me to my knees by chastening. My ingratitude is a sore and sure route to humility. How thankful I am that God does not allow me to walk in pride for very long. He lovingly takes my supposed source of pride from me. Have you seen this to be true for you, too?

God loves prayers that flow from broken and contrite hearts, and we profit most during periods of trouble and chastening. When I say we profit, I mean that our souls profit. After all, isn't that the prosperity we seek? No? Let me humbly refer you to a little book I mentioned earlier, *Wallowing in the World: a Peek at Earthly-Mindedness*. It is not well written, for heaven's sake, because I wrote it. But I trust that perhaps it will help absolve you of the notion that earthly mindedness is sensible.

James warns the rich people of this world that their corroded riches will testify against them in the end, and then he adds,

> You have lived on the earth in pleasure and luxury; you have fattened your hearts as in a day of slaughter.
> (James 5:5)

Can you see that prosperity that is designed to humble us often puffs us up instead because of our sinfulness? Prosperity ought to produce prayers of thanksgiving and praise, but the sad truth is that *smiling providences often foster self-praise, and self-confidence, which are sure to dry up "prayerful" prayer*. Then as a good father should, God then chastens, and we return to our knees, where we belong. Afflicting times are praying times. Neglecting God in prayer is more difficult in troubling times. Therefore, God sends affliction, and we are changed.

So far, we've proved that (1) prayer does not change God but (2) it does change us. There is also a third part to this equation: Does prayer change things? Take a look at the following:

> Elijah was a man with a nature like ours, and he prayed earnestly that it would not rain; and it did not rain on the land for three years and six months. And he prayed again, and the heaven gave rain, and the earth produced its fruit.
> (James 5:17-18)

It is evident that Elijah's prayers were answered. Prayer did change things. I would remind you here that in verse 16,

James had written, "The effective, fervent prayer of a righteous man avails much."

Elijah was a righteous man, although not righteous in an absolute sense. He was righteous in a gospel sense, as you and I are if we are true believers. Elijah, a man like us, then, is our example, as he and we do not love or approve of sin and iniquity.

> If I regard iniquity in my heart,
>   The Lord will not hear.
> (Psalm 66:18)

Sin impedes prayer and renders it ineffectual. We must be very circumspect about this. Our prayers must fly to God on the wings of unfeigned faith. We must look to the grace of God alone for answers to prayer and not to any pretended merit of our own.

> Elijah, a man with a nature like ours, prayed, and things changed. More things are wrought by prayer than this world dreams of.
> —Alfred, Lord Tennyson

James says that Elijah prayed "earnestly." Do I? Do you? Do we "say" prayers rather than "pray" prayers? If we do, shame on us. When we pray, are our minds fixed, our hearts burning, and our desires clear? If so, we will see our prayers change things.

You may now agree that (1) Prayer *does not* change *God*, (2) prayer *does* change *us*, and (3) prayer *does* change *things*. But you may still object that it is doubtful that God's providence fits well with these three truths about prayer. Let's see if I can pull it all together for you.

Remember secondary causes? God ordained that your fervent, effectual prayer would avail much. Could God change things without your prayer? Of course He could.

> All the inhabitants of the earth are reputed as nothing;
>
> He does according to His will in the army of heaven
> > And among the inhabitants of the earth.
> > No one can restrain His hand
> > Or say to Him, "What have you done?"
>
> (Daniel 4:35)

Do you mean to say that God could change things without my prayer but He ordains that I pray? Ah, now you see it. *God is not surprised by your earnest prayer. He ordained it.* It was integral to His plan. You offered it as an act of your free will, and God foreordained your prayer in eternity past to bring about His purpose.

> When God inclines a heart to pray,
> He hath an ear to hear.
> To Him, there's music in a groan
> And beauty in a tear.
> —William Cowper

Remember, God sovereignly overrules human action as a planned means to the accomplishment of His own goals. History is about Him, not us. We, God's creatures, are not the center of the universe; He is. There is mystery in this because of our limited understanding, but the assertion that

God controls our free actions like fervent prayer is true. The idea of His control over all of the things in His universe flabbergasts us, but it is consummately factual. God's ways, He tell us, are above our ways, and so are His thoughts.

Jephthah "spoke all his words before the LORD in Mizpah" (Judges 11:11). He demonstrated humility, dependence, gratitude, and faith. May you and I be of the same mind and spirit. I'm weary of my tepid, heartless, thoughtless prayers. It's time for me to change. I'm reminded of the lament of a character in *The Glory of the Nightingales* by E. A. Robinson: "I knew myself better, sometimes, than was a joy for me." How about you? Does your prayer life require change?

> Satan trembles when he sees the weakest saint upon his knees.
> —William Cowper

ESTHER ACCUSING HAMAN
For we are sold, I and my people, to be destroyed, to be slain, and to perish . . .
Then Haman was afraid before the king and the queen . . . (Esther 7: 4, 6)

10

Beauty Bests the Beast

Earlier I promised that we'd meet a beautiful lady who would help us to understand providence. Allow me to introduce you to the lovely Esther. Her story will demonstrate how God makes "all things work together for good to those who love God, to those who are the called according to his purpose" (Romans 8:28).

The book of Esther is the narrative of a plot, authored by the Amalekite Haman, to wipe out the Jews who had stayed behind in the land of captivity after the main body of Jews had returned to their own land. Theirs is a concurrence (remember that concept?) of providence that will most wonderfully cause the wicked Haman to be disappointed.

The name of God is not found in the book of Esther, but the *hand* of God is everywhere in it. God upholds, directs, disposes, and governs all the events, both great and small. His deliverance of the people is brought about by a series of surprising second causes. And the book is a great source of encouragement if you are in troubling and menacing times.

We shall see how God promoted Esther and Mordecai to the proper positions at the proper time to effect the deliverance of His people. All things will work together for the good of His people to bring about His purpose.

A Scripture passage I brought forth earlier bears repeating here, as it summarizes one level of the drama we find in the book of Esther.

> The wicked plots against the just,
>> And gnashes at him with his teeth.
> The Lord laughs at him,
>> For He sees that his day is coming.
> (Psalm 37:12-13)

Chapter 1 does not record the names of Esther and Mordecai, our heroine and hero. Yet the providence of God is conspicuous in laying the groundwork for Esther to rise to the position of queen, which is necessary to defeat Haman's plot against Mordecai later. A plot, I might add, that Haman hasn't even hatched as yet. God knows all, doesn't He? God controls all, doesn't He? Even evil actions and thoughts are under His control.

King Ahasuerus held a feast, and his queen, Vashti, refused to appear when the king summoned her. Vashti's refusal angered her drunken husband and his friends. Her dismissal followed, and the search for a new queen commenced. We can see that men's sins and follies serve God as He wills. *If He could not bring good out of them, they would not be permitted,* St. Augustine said.

In chapter 1, God removed the queen, and now He will elevate a very humble and obscure Jewish girl to that vacated position. His power is marvelous, isn't it? Possible brides are sought from every corner of the kingdom. Twelve months are allowed for purifying and perfuming. What extravagances worldly men undertake!

> Even those who were the masterpieces of nature must yet have all this help from art to recommend them to a vain and carnal mind.
> —Matthew Henry

We learn that Esther's parents are both dead and that her cousin, Mordecai, treats her as a daughter.

> The young woman was lovely and beautiful.
> (Esther 2:7)

Did God make her beautiful? Yes. Did it prove to be her advantage? Of course; God planned it. Our captive, Jewish orphan was born to be a queen! Only God knew it. Esther, Mordecai, and the rest had to learn it.

Mordecai, it appears, is a sort of doorkeeper in the king's court. God placed him there so that he would overhear a plot against the king. Eventually this episode will play an important role in delivering the Jews. Again, evil Haman hasn't hatched his plot yet. It is known only to God—even Haman doesn't know it.

Chapter 3 opens ominously with Haman's elevation to a high position, second only to the king in authority. Haman, the king's favorite, is to be bowed down to, and all are eager to do so except for our hero, Mordecai. On religious principal as a Jew, he will stand, but he will not bow to Haman. His refusal enrages Haman, and he plots the destruction of Mordecai and all the other Jews in the land. Thousands must die to pacify one man for another's offense? We should never underestimate the violence of prideful people.

> Of all the causes which conspire to blind
> Men's erring judgment, and misguide the mind,
> What the weak head with strongest bias rules,
> Is pride, the never-failing vice of fools.
> —Alexander Pope

An edict was sent to every region under the king's control declaring that in eleven months all of the Jews were to be killed and their goods plundered. It was a black day, but God would make it work together for good.

God's chosen people were grieved and frightened. Mordecai wept bitterly and cried throughout the city. Esther, who had become queen, inquired what the trouble was. Mordecai urged her to intercede with the king for the sparing of their people. At first Esther objected, not wanting to risk her life by going before the king when he had not called for her. But Mordecai responded with trust in God's providence:

> Do not think in your heart that you will escape in the king's palace any more than all the other Jews. For if you remain completely silent at this time, relief and deliverance will arise for the Jews from another place, but you and your father's house will perish. Yet who knows whether you have come to the kingdom for such a time as this?
> (Esther 4:13-14)

Our hero, Mordecai, demonstrated strong faith at a perilous moment. "If you remain completely silent at this time, *relief and deliverance will arise for the Jews from another place*" (italics added). Mordecai trusted God to protect the people, but he could not see how. *He reasoned that God must have elevated Esther to the throne for the very specific purpose of being the secondary cause of God's deliverance of His people:* "Who knows whether you have come to the kingdom for such a time as this?" Mordecai hazarded a guess at God's providence because he believed in God's providence. Do you view your life and its fluctuations as Mordecai did, or do you believe things "just happen"?

Esther fasted for three days and nights and then went to the king, at the peril of losing her life.

Chapter 5 opens with the king's favorable reception of Esther. Esther requested that both the king and Haman attend a banquet she had prepared for them that day. At this time, neither Haman nor the king knew that Esther was a Jew.

> At the banquet of wine the king said to Esther, "What is your petition? It shall be granted you. What is your request, up to half the kingdom? It shall be done!" (Esther 5:6)

Esther kindly entertains the king and Haman, but she delays making her request on behalf of her doomed people. Instead, she replies,

> "If it pleases the king . . . then let the king and Haman come to the banquet which I will prepare for them, and tomorrow I will do as the king has said." (Esther 5:8)

Esther's tactics demonstrate her wisdom and heighten the story's suspense. God, of course, is governing all of this. Esther's delay and holding a second banquet will allow time for Haman to lay the groundwork for his own destruction.

Haman was more full of pride that day than ever before, thinking of what a great honor the queen was showing him. Providence always finds proud men blinded by their arrogance. On his way home Haman encountered Mordecai, who still refused to bow to him. Do you think their encounter was providential? Haman was enraged and complained to his wife and friends, who suggested that Haman have a gallows built to hang Mordecai on. This seemed like a capital idea to Haman, and the gallows construction began.

Chapter 6 surprises us when God gives the king a sleepless night, during which he has books read to him. One contained the record of Mordecai's discovery of the treasonous plot mentioned at the end of chapter 2. The king inquired what honor was done Mordecai in return. Finding that nothing had been done, the king asked,

> "Who is in the court?"
> Now Haman had just entered the outer court of the king's palace to suggest that the king hang Mordecai on the gallows that he had prepared for him.
> So Haman came in, and the king asked him, "What shall be done for the man whom the king delights to honor?"
> (Esther 6:4, 6)

Haman's proud heart assumed that the king intended to honor him, and he prescribed that the honoree be dressed in royal robes, mounted on the king's own horse, and paraded around the city by one of the princes, who would continually proclaim, "Thus shall it be done to the man whom the king delights to honor!" (Esther 6:9). Oh, the hand of providence! It often provides humor while providing relief. In Haman's case, providence provided distress and confusion.

> The king said to Haman, "Hurry, take the robe and the horse, as you have suggested, and do so for Mordecai the Jew."
> (Esther 6:10)

Haman finished his task distraught, as you might imagine. God had blindsided him. His wife and friends, upon hearing how his day went, foretold his doom, which arrived in chapter 7. Providence was directing, and Haman would not escape.

The king and Haman attended Esther's second banquet. Esther explained to the king that her people were to be annihilated. The king was outraged and inquired who the monster might be who had planned this. To his face, Esther charged Haman.

Providence had cornered Haman, but a great irony was yet to surface. Ultimately the king ordered that Haman be hung upon his own gallows. Pride brought Haman down. God is always fierce against pride. God's vengeance demanded that Haman hang justly upon the very gallows he had built to unjustly hang Mordecai.

It is called God's vengeance because God providentially orchestrated all that came to pass. The men acted freely and variously, but God governed all the actions and thoughts in order that His purpose might be fulfilled. Oh, the majesty and glory we sense in even one historical narrative such as Esther's. Are you in awe? You should be.

In the beginning, I said that I hoped a glimpse at providence would alter your view of your life and all of history. Has it?

Stop and consider your life through the goggles of providence. Trace your history. Do you see and sense answers to the questions that have always gnawed at you?

For Further Consideration

Allow me a few questions about Esther's story. Please seek the parallels in your own life.

1. Ahasuerus and Haman, along with their courtiers, friends, and families, were prideful idolaters. Were they, as well as Esther and Mordecai, providentially governed?

2. Our heroine, Esther, had lost both her parents. Was providence involved in their deaths also?

3. Mordecai conjectured that God might have raised Esther to the position of queen not for her benefit, but as part of His plan to deliver His people. Do you think of life in this way?

4. Before Esther would venture to enter the king's presence at the risk of her own life, she requested that Mordecai gather the Jews who lived in Shushan for a period of prayer and fasting. She would do likewise and then go to the king. Would you have done "likewise"?

5. Mordecai's refusal to bow to proud Haman was the ruination of Haman's life, and God dealt with Haman's pride and its fruits severely. Has God providentially been resisting you and your pride?

6. In God's providence, Mordecai ended up with Haman's household and also his position at court. By the narrative's end, it's quite easy to see God's hand in all the characters' lives, especially

Mordecai's. Is it equally easy for you to see providence working in your own life?

7. The narrative begins on the heels of a long period of captivity for the Jews. Their captivity was a chastening from God. Have you been thinking about your chastenings from God?

8. Can you find even one "random" act in this narrative? One "accidental meeting"? One act of "fate"? One "lucky" turn of events? One "coincidence"?

***

1. Ahasuerus and Haman, along with their courtiers, friends, and families, were prideful idolaters. Were they, as well as Esther and Mordecai, providentially governed?

I continue asking this question in one form or another to drive home the fact that God actively governs this world and *all* of its inhabitants. *Unbelievers as well as believers go to sleep at night and awake in the morning because God sovereignly keeps them breathing through the night.* Unbelievers and believers both have the homes they have, the careers they have, and the children they have because God governs their lives.

Again, unbelievers and believers retain their free will. They court the girl they meet at the exercise club and woo her without contemplating how it happened that they were both at the same club, at the same time, on the same day. Why did they both want to use the rowing machine at the same time? If they think about it at all, they will chalk it up to chance. Even if they never acknowledge it, you and I know that God was governing their free actions.

> The LORD is good to all.
> (Psalm 145:9)
>
> [God] makes His sun rise on the evil and on the good, and sends rain on the just and on the unjust.
> (Matthew 5:45)

Sunshine and rain, in fact, are great blessings to this world. They come from God. The sun does not shine of its own accord, nor does the rain come solely by natural law. In fact, they come from God,

> Who covers the heavens with clouds,
> > Who prepares rain for the earth,
> > Who makes grass to grow on the mountains.
> He gives to the beast its food,
> > And to the young ravens that cry.
> (Psalm 147: 8-9)

Remember, natural laws are simply the normal manner in which God runs His universe. Common grace, the term we use to describe God's bringing the rain for the unjust as well as for the just, ought to provoke thanksgiving by believers and unbelievers alike. Regrettably, this proof of God's goodness is laughed at by unbelievers and is generally passed over lightly by believers.

> Since the creation of the world His invisible attributes are clearly seen, being understood by the things that are made, even His eternal power and Godhead, so that they are without excuse, because, although they

> knew God, they did not glorify Him as God, nor were thankful, but became futile in their thoughts, and their foolish hearts were darkened.
> (Romans 1:20-21)

Remember, both parties, believers and unbelievers, are utterly unworthy of any of God's blessings. They must all come by grace.

I will conclude by reminding us that all things and all men, including Ahasuerus and Haman, are provided for in this world by our gracious God. Providence is multifaceted, isn't it?

2. Our heroine, Esther, had lost both her parents. Was providence involved in their deaths also?

The staggering conclusions of a well-thought-out contemplation of providence are not lost on us, I hope. Who decides when you die? The Lord. Who decides when an Adolph Hitler or a Jeffery Dahmer dies? The Lord. Who decides when anyone dies? The Lord.

> I know that You will bring me to death.
> (Job 30:23)

Then you know who decided when Esther's parents died. God either initiates or permits all actions, right? He is either sovereign or He's not. Which is it? Remember, all actions, whether good or evil, are governed by God. Both life and death are in God's hands. The good news in your life and the bad news in your life are both in God's hands. The day of your parents' births and the day of your parents' deaths are

God's to determine. The day of *your* birth was in His hand. The day of *your* death will be as He wills. God is sovereign.

> No one has power over the spirit to retain the spirit,
> And no one has power in the day of death.
> (Ecclesiastes 8:8)

That is a thorough view of providence. *Do not amputate providence's left leg and say God has nothing to do with or control over "bad things."* Do not fall into the error of granting God the right leg of providence over "good things" only.

Was it sad when Esther's parents died? Certainly. Did they, according to normal human judgment, die prematurely? Of course. Their deaths left a young daughter without parents to train her, care for her, and raise her. Was God involved in their deaths? God is involved in all deaths. No one may die without His consent or action. Did Esther weep at her parents' burial? What do you think? Were her parents' deaths part of God's plan, His working out of history? Need I answer that for you?

The key verse for this little book is Roman's 8:28, where God is said to make all things work together for good for those who love Him and are called according to His purpose. This "all things" demands that we give providence two legs: the leg of adversity and the leg of prosperity.

Consider that every work of God is wise, just, and good. *At the end, all will appear to have been not only for the good, but for the best.* Everything that befell Esther's parents was the product of God's eternal counsel. If we are to be wise, we must consider, as Esther must have done, what God's design must be in our providences, good and bad. We must study God's design in His dealings with us if we are to be discerning and receive comfort.

3. Mordecai conjectured that God might have raised Esther to the position of queen not for her benefit, but as part of His plan to deliver His people. Do you think of life in this way?

Mordecai was directing Esther to a consideration of God's design for her life, wasn't he? If God raised her from obscurity to royalty, there was a reason for it. As I said earlier, there is wisdom in all of God's providences. That wisdom may remain unknown to us for a time before it's revealed. In fact, that wisdom may remain unknown to us to our dying day. Yet we should remain confident that the glorious wisdom of God's design will be made clear to us after our deaths.

Why were you elevated to your position in life? So that you can be self-centered? So you can drain your life away in luxury and ease? Heaven forbid! *Each of us must search for God's design in placing us where we are.* Is there a service only you can offer to God and His church? We must not allow our chance to serve our generation slip away. God has entrusted you with your position and your gifts. Use them both, and see God's providential hand guiding you. This I know: He surely is guiding you. *What you do is important.* Perhaps you are the one to speak to my son effectually. How can that happen if you're not studying hard for that "chance" meeting that you and I know is anything but chance.

There is a purpose for our lives, and I assure you the purpose is loftier than the selfish, self-centered, worldly dreams most of us have. Can we persuade ourselves to gape at providence's beauty in our lives and race to do what we were born to do? Your life has meaning, and you will find it in providence if you're wise enough to seek it.

> Timberlake to Matthias: "You told me God was dead. Matthias, you may have buried Him alive."
> —E. A. Robinson

4. Before Esther would venture to enter the king's presence at the risk of her own life, she requested that Mordecai gather the Jews who lived in Shushan for a period of prayer and fasting. She would do likewise and then go to the king. Would you have done "likewise"?

Esther determined that she would go to the king, but she first determined to go to God. She would seek the king's favor, but she would seek the Almighty's favor first.

> The king's heart is in the hand of the LORD,
>   Like the rivers of water;
>   He turns it wherever He wishes.
> (Proverbs 21:1)

Is God a prayer-hearing God? Esther thought so. Is prayer the path to God's favor? Esther proved it. Is fasting to be joined with prayer under extraordinarily difficult providences? Yes. Should friends be entreated to join with us in prayer and fasting under great trials? Wise men of all ages have followed the practice.

Why fast and pray for three days? It reminds us of our sinfulness and unworthiness. Humble, repentant beggars have always fared well with God.

Should seeking God's favor require arduous work and self-denial? If you don't think so, you are either a fool or an infant in your understanding. Folks will stay up all night for a TV get-rich-quick scheme but tire after thirty seconds of heartless prayer.

I am as guilty of years of stunted prayers as any of you are, my readers. The shame of it is real to me. Are you equally guilty? Then let's pray and repent. Let's ask God to open our eyes and hearts to His providences and purposes in our lives and in this world. Let's change and be people with a zealous, fervent prayer life. Can't the beautiful Esther be our teacher?

> Unburden'd wouldest thou be?
> Advance prayer most earnestly,
> Adorn'd with humility.
> —Author unknown

5. Mordecai's refusal to bow to proud Haman was the ruination of Haman's life, and God dealt with Haman's pride and its fruits severely. Has God providentially been resisting you and your pride?

Recently my beloved wife, Lois, took me aside to tell me how prideful I've been. Actually, she was responding to a comment I had made thanking God I wasn't as prideful as others are. Shocked doesn't accurately describe my

A man should never be ashamed to own he has been wrong, which is but saying, that he is wiser today than he was yesterday.
—Alexander Pope

response. I was closer to immobilized. It's good to have a *good* Christian wife, isn't it?

> [Jesus] spoke this parable to some who trusted in themselves that they were righteous, and despised others: "Two men went up to the temple to pray, one a Pharisee and the other a tax collector. The Pharisee stood and prayed thus with himself, 'God, I thank you that I am not like other men—extortioners, unjust, adulterers, or even as this tax collector.' . . . The tax collector, standing afar off, would not so much as raise his eyes to heaven, but beat his breast, saying, 'God, be merciful to me a sinner!' I tell you, this man went down to his house justified rather than the other; for everyone who exalts himself will be humbled, and he who humbles himself will be exalted."
> (Luke 18:9-14)

Verse 9 informs us that this parable was designed for those trusting in their own righteousness. What conceit! To believe in their own merit before God is bad enough, but to couple that with a despising of others is incredible.

The two men are going to the same place for the same reason—to pray—but how different their attitudes are. Likely the Pharisee went because it was a public place. He coveted others' eyes upon him and the silent applause he would receive for his devotion. Hypocrites so love the approval of others. The tax collector was on a mission. He had a purpose, And he gave no thought to who was watching. *The hypocrite informs God of his goodness, as if God would also applaud.* There is really not a single word of prayer in all he said; it is pure boasting. What happened to the phrase "by God's grace"? This thought is not resident in his heart, so the words will not be present upon his lips.

In contrast, humility permeates every word from the tax collector. He does not lift up either his hands or his eyes, but he does raise his heart to heaven. He smites his breast in anguish over his sin and pleads, "God, be merciful to me a sinner!" No talk of merit here, but a fear of justice rings throughout. Only mercy will do.

The tax collector is accepted; the Pharisee is not. The reason given is that God resists the proud. They are abominable to Him.

> Go, wiser thou! And in thy scale of sense,
> Weigh thy opinion against providence;
> Call imperfection what thou fancy'st such,
> Say, here he gives too little, there too much:
> Destroy all creatures for thy sport or gust,
> Yet cry, If man's unhappy, God's unjust. . . .
> Snatch from his hand the balance and the rod,
> Re-judge his justice, be the God of God.
> In pride, in reas'ning pride, our error lies;
> All quit their sphere, and rush into the skies.
> Pride still aiming at the blest abodes,
> Men would be angels, angels would be gods.
> Aspiring to be gods, if angels fell,
> Aspiring to be angels, men rebel:
> And who but wishes to invert the laws
> Of order, sins against th' eternal cause.
>
> Ask for what end the heav'nly bodies shine,

Earth for whose use? pride answers, "'Tis for mine.". . .

What would this man? Now upward will he soar,
And little less than angel, would be more;
Now looking downwards, just as griev'd appears,
To want the strength of bulls, the furs of bears. . .
Each beast, each insect, happy in its own:
Is Heav'n unkind to man, and man alone?
—Alexander Pope, *Essay on Man,* epistle 1

> God resists the proud, but gives grace to the humble. (1 Peter 5:5)

My beloved Lois was right about me. I was never more a prideful Pharisee. If I didn't guard against my pride, I'd soon be receiving another reproof from God through the woman I adore.

What about you? Is it possible that you're unaware that pride drapes you like a cheap robe? Search yourself, and then ask your spouse or someone else close to you to search for it in you too. *Pride, glasses, and lint are three things more easily found by our spouses or friends than by us.*

Haman was exceedingly proud that the queen had invited him to the banquet. *What a trio,* he thought. *The queen, the king, and I.* Splendid thoughts of self test us at all times, but Haman had surrendered to them long before.

Self-admirers are self-deceivers. The queen was not inviting Haman to a banquet but rather to the bar of justice.

Haman passed Mordecai, and Mordecai would not bow. Mordecai trusted that God would providentially deliver him and the others. He would not mollify Haman to gain favor. Haman was enraged.

> A proud and haughty man—"Scoffer" is his name;
> > He acts with arrogant pride.
> (Proverbs 21:24)

Has any man ever answered better to this verse than Haman? Perhaps you and I are Haman's equal in this matter of pride. I hope not, but I fear it may be true. If you are too prideful for self-examination and spousal or pastoral examination, then you are probably Haman's progeny.

Does God seem to be providentially resisting you? Perhaps it's your pride. Ask someone strong and wise to examine you. Every boil must be lanced before it can be healed. Sort of sobering to think of my pride as a boil needing to be lanced, don't you think?

6. In God's providence, Mordecai ended up with Haman's household and also his position at court. By the narrative's end, it's quite easy to see God's hand in all the characters' lives, especially Mordecai's. Is it equally easy for you to see providence working in your own life?

The purpose of this book is to drive you to a daily musing on providence in your life. I will say it over and over until it sinks in: A contemplation of providence will either make you the wisest person on your block or the one perceived to be the craziest. A proper understanding of providence alters your view of your life, everyone else's life, and history.

You are significant. God is governing you for a reason. Since all His reasons are wise, you're certainly being governed wisely for a wise end. Life is short and full of both adversity and prosperity. You may remember that Ecclesiastes 7:14 called them the day of adversity and the day of prosperity. That's apropos, as both are short and one is easily and quickly exchanged for the other. Today we are the "haves." Tomorrow we'll be the "have-nots." God wisely weaves both into our lives because the balance is best for us as believers.

If you haven't spent time—serious time—considering God's purpose in placing you where you are today, you should. What could you be doing that's more important? Only a consideration of providence can permit you an understanding of all the facets of your life. Why do you exist at all? What molding have you undergone? For what purpose? *Providence makes your pain purposeful. The great Sculptor has been shaping you. Wouldn't you like to know why?* I promise you'll be energized by a reflection on God's providences in your life. You have God's eye, and now He has your ear. What service is ahead for you? Whom will you meet tomorrow through God's hand? Perhaps the most important person you'll ever meet?

Recognition of God's governance of your life will also make prayer and Bible study a pleasure.

7. The narrative begins on the heels of a long period of captivity for the Jews. Their captivity was a chastening from God. Have you been thinking about your chastenings from God?

Our second foundational text for this little book is Hebrews 12:5, which promises believers that God will chasten those He loves. He has never deviated from this practice in the past, and He won't in the future.

Verse 10 assures us that God chastens us for our profit, if we are believers, so that "we may be partakers of His holiness" (Hebrews 12:10). Romans 8:29 styles it being "conformed to the image of His son."

Hebrews 12 also promises that God's chastening will be painful. Let's be thankful it comes from a loving hand!

> We are now between the hammer and the anvil.
> —Thomas Watson

Have you reviewed your life with an eye to providence in your past sufferings since we first discussed Hebrews 12? I hope you have. We all wish to understand our lives, don't we—especially our pain? You want that special suffering to be purposeful, don't you? Only in God's providence will you find answers for the questions Jimmy Buffet's dad lived with, as I mentioned before, the "questions that bothered him so," in the song titled "He Went to Paris."

Final Thought

Jeremiah, the weeping prophet, witnessed the sufferings of God's people. In fact, he suffered greatly with them for their sins. Providence cast His covenant people into grievous captivity justly because of their sin and lovingly for their chastening.

> "They have bent their tongues for lies.
> They are not valiant for the truth on the earth.
> For they proceed from evil to evil,
> And they do not know me," says the LORD. . . .
> They have taught their tongue to speak lies;
> They weary themselves to commit iniquity.
> (Jeremiah 9:3-5)

Sin was rampant in Israel in Jeremiah's day, much as it is in America in our day. Jeremiah unsuccessfully attempted to convict the people of their sinful ways, but *the religious leaders persuaded the people that God would never chasten them. After all,* they reasoned, *God loves us!* Sounds eerily familiar, doesn't it? How many pastors today scoff at the notion that God would chasten His church?

It is remarkably easy to be deceived about chastening. Perhaps that's due to the fact that we all wish to avoid pain. Even when we are assured it's beneficial to us, we often are zealous to live pain-free lives. Disheartening as it may be, I confess to you that I still find my heart longs to live free of pain. I haven't the courage to say to God, "Do what you need to do to make me more like Christ, even if it requires endless pain." Perhaps someday I'll be wise enough to utter that simple prayer and mean it.

Could God possibly be chastening you for your sin? The one you love so dearly? No? Then perhaps God is trying you as he did Job to prove your faith. Either way, if you are facing a stern chastening or trial, then rejoice. There is nothing more glorifying to God than a suffering saint who accepts his or her chastening agreeably, confident that it is from the Father's wise and loving hand.

> The real problem is not why some pious, humble, believing people suffer, but why some do not.
> —C. S. Lewis

Remember, through our chastenings God is conforming us to the image of His son:

> My brethren, count it all joy when you fall into various trials, knowing that the testing of your faith produces patience.
> (James 1:2-3)

Gold is perfected by fire, and so are you and I.

> Poor mortal man cannot afford
> to have his sorrows cease,
> for they prepare his locked-in soul
> for sweet and sure release.
> —H. C. Carlisle

8. Can you find even one "random" act in this narrative? One "accidental meeting"? One act of "fate"? One "lucky" turn of events? One "coincidence"?

The third of our foundational Scripture passages is 1 Kings 22, which refutes the idea that anything happens by chance. Why was Esther born when she was? Why to those particular parents? Why not to others? Why was she born beautiful? How did Mordecai come to be her relative? How did Mordecai come to be her guardian?

It's simple to ask the same questions of your life. *Do you ask them?* Have you ever considered why you have the parents you do? Why weren't you born in 1865 near the close of the Civil War? Others were born the day Lincoln was assassinated, weren't they? Could you have switched places with them without affecting history? Can you see that you were sovereignly chosen to be born to your particular parents on your particular birthday? Couldn't your mother have married someone else? She wanted to, you know.

Your mother and father freely chose each other, just as the Syrian archer freely drew his bow and launched his arrow. Just as freely, God governed the courtship of your mother and the destination of the Syrian's arrow.

Does awe creep over you? *This is how the world actually works.* This is how your life is unfolding. *Chance, fate, and random events are nonsense and nonexistent.* The Bible pointedly teaches our free will and God's sovereignty side by side. Since all Scripture is "God-breathed," we may trust this view of our lives, even if we can't fully understand it.

What a marvelous door of understanding is unlocked with the key of providence!

THE FINDING OF MOSES
And when she [the daughter of Pharaoh] had opened it, she saw the child: and, behold, the babe wept. And she had compassion on him, and said, This is one of the Hebrews' children . . . (Exodus 2: 6)

11

A Command As Rigorous As It Was Cruel

> Pharaoh commanded all his people, saying, "Every son who is born you shall cast into the river, and every daughter you shall save alive."
> (Exodus 1:22)

As I've said before, all of history truly is God's story. Moses, the penman of the book of Exodus, is also its hero, but the story is God's.

God had determined that Moses would be a type of Christ, a lawgiver, a mediator, and a statesman. Was there any chance that a Pharaoh's edict could or would countermand God's? Was there any chance that Moses would be drowned? All of the participants in the drama—Pharaoh, Moses' mother and sister, and all the others—were governed by God to produce the end He desired. Yet none of the participants were aware that God was governing every word and every action. Sounds like our lives, doesn't it?

Undoubtedly, many perished as a result of Pharaoh's order that the sons should be slain, but not Moses. God providentially permitted the other infants to die, while he spared Moses. Is that fair? Fallen human beings that we are, we always have that question on the tips of our tongues. Let me ask you, before you, a creature, prosecute the eternal Creator, will not the Judge of the whole earth do right?

Do we accuse God, who is perfection itself, of injustice? We are the sinful spawn of sinful lineage running from our fathers back to Adam, and do we accuse the Lord of glory of unfairness? God does not owe you or me or the infants drowned at Pharaoh's command one more breath, let alone an explanation we'll understand. Why am I so harsh? Because in foolishness, I waxed rhapsodic about God's being unfair when I was first converted. (At that point, I didn't have Lois to keep me from being stupid.) Now you have me to stop you from being as foolish and impertinent as I was. Your present breath, as well as mine, is a gift of God's grace and mercy. God is perfectly good and perfectly wise in all His dealings with all His creatures.

Observe the grandeur of providence: A deliverer would be needed many years hence, so he is born now, when the notion of a deliverer was in no one's mind except God's.

Was it providential that Moses was more than ordinarily beautiful?

> When [Moses' mother] saw that he was a beautiful child, she hid him three months.
> (Exodus 2:2)

When Moses' mother saw that he was beautiful and healthy, she hid him at the peril of her own life. After three months, she could hide him no longer. She had to lean on providence. She placed Moses in an ark made of bulrushes and set him afloat by the riverbank with his sister watching from a distance.

> His sister stood afar off, to know what would be done to him. (Exodus 2:4)

His sister did not know what would happen; she had to wait to find out. God knew. Every event is known to Him and always has been. God put it into their hearts to put Moses into the ark in order to bring about His purpose.

Moses the baby was to fall into the Pharaoh's daughter's hands so that Moses the future deliverer of Israel would be perfectly qualified, educated, and situated to deliver God's people from the Pharaoh's grasp when the proper time came.

Imagine the scene and all the players, if you will. The sister hiding and watching, the mother at an even farther distance, and the Pharaoh's daughter strolling by the river with her entourage.

Imagine it from the sister's vantage point, and consider the disquieting number of possibilities. Is the basket watertight? Moses is so tiny. How long can he survive in the sun? He's only three month old. How long can he endure without water and food? What if the current sweeps him away? What of the crocodiles? Will Moses' big sister have to watch her baby brother torn to pieces by one of those ancient predators with those dead eyes?

What of hidden rocks and branches? The weeds are tall. What if no one sees him? What if soldiers discover him? Will they drown him? What if another Egyptian woman with a tender heart chances upon Moses? She will have to drown him. It has been commanded! What if the Pharaoh's daughter, the kingdom's only candidate to save Moses, doesn't feel well today and skips her walk by the river?

Here she comes. Can you imagine the sister's heart rate? Providence guided the Pharaoh's daughter to the river exactly when she needed to be there. She was guided to exactly the place on the riverbank where Moses lay quietly.

A maid fetches the basket, pulls back the covering and—the baby cries.

Undoubtedly the Pharaoh's daughter was moved with compassion and probably also by the baby's beauty. Moses' sister ventures forth to inquire if a Hebrew nurse ought to be sought for the Hebrew infant. Moses' own mother becomes his nurse. Need I press you to weigh how all these circumstances could be brought together? Do God's power and wisdom move you?

> The lengthened shadow of a man is history, said Emerson.
> —T. S. Eliot

Emerson was never more wrong. The lengthened shadow of a man is *His story,* God's story.

For Further Consideration

1. God watched over Moses so tenderly and closely. Did He watch over you with the same vigilance when you were an infant?

2. Consider your life from five to fifteen. Was providence guarding and guiding you?

3. Moses seemed marked for obscurity, if not for death. What is your case? Were you born into poverty to worthless parents? Is that a hindrance to God's making great use of you?

4. The Pharaoh's daughter "chanced by"? Are you persuaded now that there are no "chance" meetings, no "coincidences"? In your life, have there been "chance" meetings that you now see weren't by chance at all?

5. Moses was, at all points in his early life, being prepared by God for a task that would come decades later. Could this be true of your life?

***

1. God watched over Moses so tenderly and closely. Did He watch over you with the same vigilance when you were an infant?

Praise ought to rise to our lips instantly as we ponder the providential care we received as infants. Perils abound in infancy. Why did we escape them? A mother's care? A secondary cause. Who selected your mother for you? Who gave you a caring mother? Praise ought to overflow to our sovereign Maker.

What a flood of providential occurrences have gone unpraised in my life. I strain to remember stories, and a few special rescues come to my mind. Why did two boys, one seven and one three, have access to a gun anyway? Why did one take a bullet to the stomach while the other exited unscathed? Why does a lad who cannot swim venture into deep water, only to slip off his inner tube? Under for the third time as the crowd's shrieks gave way to the lonesome silence of the water—wait—my father, a former Navy frogman, was ill and near the shore rather than away at the ball field. He dove in and saved me. Coincidence? No, providence!

Some events in our lives are so clearly special providences that other explanations defy logic. Let me relate one of these for you.

At one point in my life, Fridays meant lunch at a greasy spoon with my friend George. Fried catfish was their specialty, and we never considered ordering anything else. George had mastered bone removal. With one stroke the bone and the meat would be parted. Each Friday brought another attempt on my part to master the one-stroke-bone-removal technique, and each Friday the attempt failed. Of course, my failures did not make the fish any less delectable.

One sunny, spring Friday found us chatting away, as we always did, like two old charwomen. Suddenly I could barely draw a breath! My continued gulping was disturbing. Precious little air was reaching my lungs. George, seeing my distress, shoved the bread basket in my direction. I grabbed a piece and swallowed it, hoping to dislodge the bone I was certain was blocking my windpipe. (Your mother may have taught you the same remedy.)

There was no improvement. I remembered not to panic, but I was concerned and light-headed. Waitresses clustered like death angels, and Jerry, the owner, hovered, probably fearing a lawsuit. Did I mention George was an attorney? Jerry had reason to worry. Nothing and no one helped relieve my trouble.

I determined that I could breathe, and it appeared unlikely I'd pass out, so I foolishly decided to drive myself to the emergency room. Have you noticed that every one of these stories includes one or two foolish actions on my part? George followed me, and I arrived safely at the hospital. Walking in under my own power was difficult, but I managed.

My distress registered with the hospital staff, and they quickly rushed me into an examining room. My whisper was audible, but barely. Quickly a handful of doctors and would-be doctors surrounded me. A long steel apparatus with a mirror attached was inserted into my throat, and the culprit bone appeared to have little chance of survival.

"Mr. Moore, I believe there's a bone lodged in your windpipe." This did precious little to bolster my confidence, as I had whispered that diagnosis to the admitting nurse.

After twenty minutes of close-up breathing by the gaggle of doctors, I'd had my fill. "Enough."

"Mr. Moore, even with this apparatus (he actually called it by a very scientific and fine-sounding name, as doctors are prone to do) we are unable to see anything. Perhaps it's been dislodged."

"I can feel it," I whispered. "I can barely breathe."

"Yes, we noticed, but we now feel it's psychosomatic. Your throat is sore, and you're just reacting as if the impediment is still there."

"You're a moron!" I have about twenty-five ways of saying this, emphasizing one syllable or another. It's good that I do, as I am not clever enough to come up with an alternative "exasperated reply."

"Don't upset yourself, Mr. Moore, it will not help."

"Is your dad available?"

"What do you mean?"

"Get me somebody more experienced and brighter than you are," I croaked out.

At just that moment (all stories about providence have a place for that phrase), a nerdy-looking little fellow meandered in. He was whisperingly apprised of my dilemma and attitude. Gingerly, he offered, "Mr. Moore, by chance, there is a man lecturing in the main hall right now whose specialty is the removal of fish bones from throats. Would you like me to get him?"

I'll skip my response, which was less than Christian.

Within a few minutes, while I struggled for shallow breaths surrounded by enough doctors to field a bowling team, a swarthy, angular man in his forties walked in.

In broken English (he was from Argentina) he announced himself. "Sir, I'm Dr. So-and-so. Are you a God-fearing man by chance? I ask because I'm about to show you an instrument that these men have never seen." With that he reached for a black case that looked like it might conceal a cue stick. It clicked open and revealed an odd instrument with multiple mirrors and attachments.

"Sir, there are but two of these instruments in the world. One is in my office at home, and the other is here. That is why I asked if you're a God-fearing man."

"Yeah, but I'm not Catholic." Why I answered that way is beyond me. I guess I just assumed all Argentineans were Catholic.

Dr. So-and-so laughed and continued. "Sir, if I weren't here, these other fellows would next perform a tracheotomy. Do you know what that is?"

I nodded. "They think it's psychosomatic," I tattled.

That made him roar with delight. "Sir, I assure you it's not psychosomatic. Your airway is blocked. We shall find out what it is."

Assembling the instrument took only a few seconds. It sort of snapped together.

"Sir, I will need to inject your throat with something that will relax your impulse to gag. Do you understand?"

I nodded again.

Within minutes the offending fishbone had been located and extracted. This doctor's instrument with its multiple mirrors was capable of looking farther down my throat than the hospital's instrument could. One was a Honda Civic; the other was a Maserati.

I could see the bone on the monitor, as his instrument contained a video camera. The bone had punctured both sides of my esophagus and was perched there sort of wishbone-like. How the bread ever passed by it I have no idea. (By the way, the doctor informed me that Mom was wrong. Never try to dislodge a fishbone by gulping down a hunk of bread. It only increases the chance you'll imbed the bone. Thanks, Mom.)

Dr. So-and-so withdrew his instrument once, attached a scissorlike tip to it, and reinserted it into my throat. He easily clipped the bone where it had penetrated both sides of my esophagus and sent me on my way.

Coincidence or providence? Just two of those instruments in the entire world, and one found its way, at exactly the precise time I needed it, to Springfield, Illinois. Did God send the Argentine doctor? Of course. Was the doctor aware of his mission? No, he came to lecture. Did I mention that the reason there were only two of these instruments in the world was because Dr. So-and-so was the inventor?

As I left, the doctor shook my hand and said, "Sir, do you know that I arrived at precisely eleven o'clock to lecture and that my plane leaves at two? If you had come later, your throat would have been opened, and you'd be breathing through a tube. And those doctors still would not have seen the bone."

I told him I was the God-fearing man he had guessed I was.

Each of you, when you scan your memory bank, will find similar evidence of providential care in your life. What of the care we're not cognizant of? Consider the trips in your family car to the Ozarks. Why did the car one-half mile ahead wreck and not your dad's car?

Why did your dad's Buick's front tire blow out, sending you into the median and safety as your family raced up Pike's Peak? Couldn't the Buick have rammed a concrete pillar at the overpass? Couldn't the Buick have slammed into a semi full of lumber? Couldn't the Buick have tumbled over the cliff and down the side of the mountain? In heaven we will have disclosed to us just how personal God's care has been in our lives.

Providence makes you reconsider your life, doesn't it?

> You formed my inward parts;
>> You covered me in my mother's womb.
> I will praise You, for I am fearfully and wonderfully made;
>> Marvelous are your works. . . .
> My frame was not hidden from You
>> When I was made in secret. . . .
> Your eyes saw my substance, being yet unformed.
>> And in Your book they all were written,
>> The days fashioned for me.
>> When as yet there were none of them.
> (Psalm 139:13-16)

I mention these verses again because I want you to dwell on the idea that the days of your life, the ones fashioned for you, were written in His book before time began. Some ideas need to be pondered; others need to be dwelt upon.

2. Consider your life from five to fifteen. Was providence guarding and guiding you?

Most people I speak with can quickly and easily rattle off the painful experiences of their youths. Classmates sneering at your dress? Disparaging remarks about your broken and crooked teeth? Crushing comments concerning your freckles? The buzzing about your birthmark?

Pause a moment, please, and whisper quietly to yourself your list of hurtful recollections. Is that difficult? Are the wounds still too fresh, even after all these years? Is all that meaningless misery still chafing your poor heart?

What if you were to survey your life through the eyes of providence?

> God gets His best soldiers from the Highlands of affliction.
> —C. H. Spurgeon

Can you see that the meaningless misery I mentioned above is misnamed? For a believer, God makes "all things" to work together for good. He gives meaning to everything that happens. The Potter takes every snide comment, every cruel sneer, and all of the piercing reproaches and uses them to mold the clay into something beautiful.

> Affliction is not sent in vain, young man, from that good God who chastens whom He loves.
> —R. Southey

The pain has been profitable for you. The heaviness, the weeping, and the humiliation all shaped you for His service. *This Potter permits no unnecessary pain, for believers. You have not suffered needlessly.* The angels view our worlds through the eyes of providence. Can we?

If you're an unbeliever, God has not promised to make "all things" work together for your good. Your suffering here is only a prelude to your eternal suffering.

> They shall go forth and look
> Upon the corpses of the men
> Who have transgressed against Me.
> For their worm does not die
> And their fire is not quenched.
> They shall be an abhorrence to all flesh.
> (Isaiah 66:24)

The eternal heartache that awaits you will cause you to long for the agony you now hide away. I'm being plain because I hope you will weary of fighting against your own best interests. Surrender your bravado, fall to your knees, and bow to Him who has given you every breath you've ever taken.

> Oh come, let us worship and bow down;
> Let us kneel before the LORD our Maker,
> For He is our God.
> (Psalm 95:6-7)

As swift as people are to rattle off the painful experiences of their youths, they are conversely sluggish in recounting the providential care they received before their late teen years. This is true of believers as well as unbelievers. God has sculpted you at times with the flat blade of unwarranted criticism. At other times He has transformed you by the loving praise of your blessed mother. The encouraging teachers, the thoughtful clergyman, the passionate baker who took a special interest in you, and the aunt who admired your grit, were all on assignment from God. Were they aware of it? Probably not. But they were also knives in the hands of the Master Sculptor, used to shape you when you needed it as you spun round and round on the Potter's wheel.

> Soon the mallet and chisel sharp
> the stubborn block assailed,
> And blow by blow, and pang by pang,
> The prisoner unveiled.
> —Anonymous

If we were wise, we'd thank God for both the good news and the bad news in our lives. As believers, we've been shaped by both. The Sculptor has shaped us by making all things work together for our good. The sad truth is that in most Christian's lives, I find ingratitude to be a giant and gratitude to be a dwarf. Perhaps I'm speaking primarily about my own life. *Ingratitude is a far greater sin than we realize.* What do you and I have that wasn't given us? I am talking only about good news here. I'm not asking us to be mature and thank God for the bad news He's made work for our souls' best interests. How often have we stolen God's glory and deprived Him of His rightful praise by taking to ourselves the credit that belongs to Him?

> Who makes you differ from another? And what do you have that you did not receive? Now, if you did indeed receive it, why do you boast as if you had not received it?
> (1 Corinthians 4:7)

God's care is and always has been constant in our lives. Gratitude opens heaven to us as quickly as ingratitude closes it. Our providential care should cause us to gush forth God's praises. "All things" have been made to serve us. This is how the world truly works. It is understood only through the spectacles of providence. May we praise God now and forevermore. Our pain has been meaningful, not meaningless. God's fatherly care has been constant as well as tender. Each of your happinesses and successes are directly attributable to His hand. There has been and is a purpose in all the things that have befallen you. God's purpose stands behind it all.

3. Moses seemed marked for obscurity, if not for death. What is your case? Were you born into poverty to worthless parents? Is that a hindrance to God's making great use of you?

What a marvelous door of understanding is unlocked with the key of providence!

Providence allows us to see that God has a purpose in history. Our personal histories are part of the fabric of His eternal purpose. It is difficult for us to view all of history and all of humankind from this vantage point, but we must learn to. Once the edict was given that the Hebrew male children must be destroyed, Moses appeared to be doomed.

His humble birth in a foreign land would most assuredly be immediately followed by his tiny lungs being filled with the cold waters of the Nile. What an inauspicious birth and obscure death seemed to await him.

The Scriptures permits us to perceive the events of Moses' life differently, don't they? We learn that God had a purpose for this baby. He was to be the deliverer of God's people decades in the future. The edict could not defeat God's purpose. The edict, in truth, was a key element in bringing about God's purpose.

The Scriptures are flush with biographies of men and women born in anonymity, often of scandalous or worthless parents. In fact, God seems to delight in elevating the least promising and most unlikely men and women to high places, for high purposes. We've already met Esther and Jephthah, whose lives certainly fit this bill. Please let me introduce you to another man of lowly birth who is now great in the history of heaven.

> I was no prophet,
> Nor was I a son of a prophet,
> But I was a sheepbreeder
> And a tender of sycamore fruit.
> (Amos 7:14)

Although Amos's background was rural and his dwelling far from the centers of learning, God selected and groomed Amos to speak for Him. In a land filled with professional clergy, Amos, a sheepherder, was divinely chosen to prophesy harsh things in the king's sanctuary.

> The LORD took me as I followed the flock,
> And the LORD said to me,

> "Go, prophesy to My people Israel."
> (Amos 7:15)

God sometimes chooses the foolish things of the world to confound the wise (see 1 Corinthians 1:27). The contemplative work of being a shepherd produced David and Moses as well.

Origins and beginnings that are humble ought not to be a barrier to service if God has endowed people with ability. Amos had nothing to be ashamed of, even if others censured him for being a shepherd.

Amos was a plain countryman, used to country work, now called to prophesy at a king's court. Elisha was called while he was behind a plough, and what are we to say of those poor fisherman the Lord chose to be his closest companions? Andrew, Peter, James, and John were unlearned men who were transformed by being with Jesus:

> When they saw the boldness of Peter and John, and perceived that they were uneducated and untrained men, they marveled. And they realized that they had been with Jesus.
> (Acts 4:13)

> We have this treasure in earthen vessels, that the excellence of the power may be of God and not of us.
> (2 Corinthians 4:7)

It is God's way to work through those who are weak or unimpressive in the world's eyes. God often uses ordinary people. Amos, a herdsman of Tekoa, puts to shame a court-practicing priest of Bethel.

Obscure births, rascals for parents, and out-of-the-way locales are no fence to our doing great works for God, provided God gives the ability. Sovereignty and providence are clear in Amos's life. God's sovereignty and providence are equally clear in your life, to those who have eyes to see.

4. The Pharaoh's daughter "chanced by"? Are you persuaded now that there are no "chance" meetings, no "coincidences"? In your life, have there been "chance" meetings that you now see weren't by chance at all?

Did the Pharaoh's daughter "chance" by? From her perspective she freely awoke, freely dressed, and arose for a leisurely walk to the river to bathe.

Did she know she was on a divine mission? No. Did she worship the God she was performing a service for? No. Was God still able to ensure that Pharaoh's daughter would be there when baby Moses needed her? Dazzling, isn't it?

The Pharaoh's cruel edict that all male Hebrew babies be cast into the river did not keep God's chosen deliverer, Moses, from being safe. In fact, Israel's future deliverer was to be raised by the Pharaoh's own daughter! Providence is beautiful.

Our lives are in God's hands. How else can one understand this? Your life is as governed by God as Moses' life was? *Has anything happened by "chance" in your life? I think you know better.*

Review your life. Think of the important folks you've met due to "chance" meetings. What if they weren't "chance" meetings? What if God governed all those "chance" meetings? He did, you know. Is there a purpose in these "chance" meetings? You know there is.

5. Moses was, at all points in his early life, being prepared by God for a task that would come decades later. Could this be true of your life?

It would be decades before Moses would understand God's wisdom in having him found by Pharaoh's daughter. Might that be so in your life? What a wonderful idea to contemplate. Now contemplate, if you dare, the God behind this wonderful idea to contemplate.

Many of you who were born in poverty and marked for obscurity were truly being prepared for a service you've yet to render. Providence often makes rulers of the least likely candidates. God delights to do this because it so clearly demonstrates His power. God prepared Moses by having him educated at court. How fitting, as Moses was later to be God's ambassador to that court.

Please, stop long enough to take a close look at your life. I love to hear the details of folks' lives, as any fair-minded person can see the divine hand at work in everyone's life. Why would you search for significance anywhere but in God's plan? You are, indeed, part of His story.

There are no accidents, all things have a deep and calculated purpose; sometimes the methods employed by Providence seem strange and incongruous, but we have only to be patient and wait for the result. Then we recognize that no others would have answered the purpose, and we are rebuked and humbled.
—Mark Twain

12

I Can't See What God's Doing— Isn't That Important?

The Bible's classic lesson on providence is found in the life of Jacob's son Joseph:

> Now Israel loved Joseph more than all his children, because he was the son of his old age. Also he made him a tunic of many colors. But when his brothers saw that their father loved him more than all his brothers, they hated him. (Genesis 37: 3-4)

From a human perspective, we are encountering a family plagued by jealousy. The improvident favoritism of Jacob (Israel) for Joseph galled his brothers, and they hated Joseph. Why did they hate him? Because Joseph informed his father of their wickedness. Because Jacob loved Joseph more than he loved his other sons. Because Jacob made Joseph a splendid tunic. Because Joseph dreamed of his dominion over his brothers. While the brothers' jealousy is somewhat understandable, their cruelty is not.

They determined to slay Joseph but then relented and decided to starve him by throwing him into a pit and leaving him there. But their plan changed, and Joseph was sold into slavery. The brothers aggravated the crime by making their father believe that Joseph was torn to pieces by wild animals. *All of this was working together for good, especially for the wicked brothers.*

God had a purpose that no one in the drama could comprehend. The brothers' guilt is obvious, as is Jacob's anguish. He did lose his son. A bewildered Joseph was sold as a slave and purchased by Potiphar. And all of these people and events were under God's control.

Did Joseph understand that his present humiliation would lead to his future exaltation? Of course not. How could he? Yet it was always true that God would raise Joseph to a leadership position so that when the famine came two decades later, Joseph would be able to provide food for the same brothers who had sold him into slavery.

> There are no accidents, all things have a deep and calculated purpose; sometimes the methods employed by Providence seem strange and incongruous, but we have only to be patient and wait for the result. Then we recognize that no others would have answered the purpose, and we are rebuked and humbled.
> —Mark Twain

How astonishing and intriguing is this family drama? Does your family's history have its share of duplicitous dealings and wicked ways? Can God work "all things" together for good in your case? If you are a believer, you have God's word that He will. We should gaze at our lives now, knowing that in our darkness we aren't able to see clearly the workings of providence. But rest assured, in heaven we shall see precisely what God's purpose was in letting our lives fall out as they have and will.

Joseph's Egyptian owner was a man named Potiphar, an officer of Pharaoh. Because God's providence was at work, through Potiphar, Joseph came in contact with public persons and public business. This would serve him well later when his time of preferment arrived.

> Providence is to be acknowledged in the disposal even of poor servants and in their settlements, and therein may perhaps be working towards something great and important.
> —Matthew Henry

God prospered Joseph and was with him even though Joseph was a slave in a foreign land. Joseph rose to the position of overseer. The household came under Joseph's authority, and God prospered the Egyptian Potiphar for Joseph's sake. Providence honored him.

Providence, likewise, governed what happened in the remainder of Genesis 39. Potiphar's wife falsely accused Joseph of attacking her. In fact, Joseph had fled her chamber to escape her wantonness. She slandered Joseph to his fellow servants and lied to her husband about Joseph's conduct, and an angry Potiphar had Joseph placed in the king's prison. *"Good things" and "bad things" are all under God's government, aren't they?*

Joseph, with God's permission, languished in prison, but not forever.

> The LORD was with Joseph and showed him mercy, and He gave him favor in the sight of the keeper of the prison.
> (Genesis 39:21)

Joseph shortly rose to second in command in the king's prison, which, providentially, brought him into contact with key players in his drama.

What do you suppose Joseph thought of all this? The years were clicking off, and his suffering continued. He had done nothing wrong. Do you think he might have speculated about God's plan for him? He surely could not have guessed what God had in store for him. Neither can we. We must imitate Joseph and be faithful and leave the rest to God's infinite wisdom. There was a purpose in Joseph's suffering, just as there is in yours and mine.

Providence brought about Joseph's advancement in unusual ways. There were key prisoners to meet, dreams to be interpreted, and further imprisonment to be endured. Yet God was governing all, and His purpose was being served.

> It came to pass, at the end of two full years, that Pharaoh had a dream.
> (Genesis 41:1)

God sovereignly caused Pharaoh to dream, just as He had kept the king from sleeping in the story of Esther. How else can it be understood? God's control extends to unbelievers, both their thoughts and their walks.

The Pharaoh's chief butler, who had met this obscure young man Joseph in prison, recommended him to interpret the Pharaoh's dream. Joseph was quickly summoned and proceeded to explain to Pharaoh what God was about to do. God would bring seven years of plenty followed by seven years of famine. Joseph counseled Pharaoh to appoint a man over the land of Egypt to collect one-fifth of the produce in the seven plentiful years and store it away for the lean years.

Joseph further suggested that Pharaoh "select a discerning and wise man" (Genesis 41:33).

Pharaoh, recognizing Joseph's wisdom and grace, told him,

> "You shall be over my house, and all my people shall be ruled according to your word; only in regard to the throne will I be greater than you."
> (Genesis 41:40)

Joseph's preferment was as wonderfully unimaginable as it was sudden. Providence had imprisoned Joseph and now it was promoting him—and all through the actions of ungodly men.

Joseph would wait a few additional years to see God's ultimate purpose revealed. Again, how could he have understood that this wasn't the end of his story? We must apply the same question to our own lives.

God sovereignly provided the promised seven years of plenty, followed by a time of famine.

In due time, Jacob sent his sons to Egypt to secure grain. And although they met Joseph face-to-face, they did not recognize him. But Joseph was put in remembrance of the long-ago dream God had given him that his family would pay homage to him.

The next few chapters of Genesis record Joseph's interaction with his brothers and his testing of their character and intent. Finally, Joseph could no longer contain himself and his joy.

> Joseph said to his brothers, "I am Joseph; does my father still live?" But his brothers could not answer

> him, for they were dismayed in his presence. . . . "I am Joseph your brother, who you sold into Egypt. But now, do not therefore be grieved or angry with yourselves because you sold me here; for God sent me before you to preserve life. . . . God sent me before you to preserve a posterity for you in the earth, and to save your lives by a great deliverance. So now it was not you who sent me here, but God."
> (Genesis 45: 3-8)

Joseph sought to soothe his brothers' fears by teaching them that whatever evil they had intended in selling him, God had intended it for good. No thanks to them for their wicked plans, but all praise to God, who has the power to make "all things" work for good. God knows the beginning and the end alike; we do not. Those who had sold Joseph into slavery were reaping the benefit that God brought out of it. They schemed to defeat Joseph's dream by selling him into Egypt, but God used the same action to confirm and establish Joseph's dream.

Jacob trekked to Egypt for a glorious reunion with the son he thought was dead. The family prospered in Egypt, but when Jacob died, his death reignited the brothers' fears that Joseph would repay them for the evil they had done to him.

> Joseph said to them, "Do not be afraid, for am I in the place of God? But as for you, you meant evil against me; but God meant it for good."
> (Genesis 50: 19-20)

Providence often uses men's performances in a way they didn't imagine. People mean one thing, God means another, and His desire stands. God often brings good out of evil, even out of the sins of men.

Have you found this to be true in your life? *Was what others designed to injure you later seen to be a blessing? Only God can do this.* Providence is invigorating, isn't it? God, in infinite wisdom and power, overrules all events and people in a way that gives Him praise and honor. For believers, as it was for Joseph, "all things" work together for good.

For Further Consideration

1. God in His providence was involved in every aspect and detail of Joseph's life. As Joseph finally recognized, God had sent Joseph to Egypt. Are the brothers who sold him into slavery guiltless then? After all, they were integral to God's plan.

2. What if Joseph had not related the two dreams he had as a youth to his brothers? Would history have been altered?

3. Was Joseph aware that God's "invisible hand" was directing his life the day he was sold to Potiphar?

4. Joseph rose to an elevated position in Potiphar's household. Later, he also rose in responsibility while he was in prison. Finally, he became the second most important man in Egypt. What part of these advancements should be attributed to God, and what part should be attributed to Joseph?

5. Pharaoh had a dream. How does God cause an unbeliever such as Pharaoh to dream anything?

6. Jacob bewails his fate in Genesis 42:36: "You have bereaved me: Joseph is no more, Simeon is no more, and you want to take Benjamin. All these things are against me." Was he wrong?

***

1. God in His providence was involved in every aspect and detail of Joseph's life. As Joseph finally recognized, God had sent Joseph to Egypt. Are the brothers who sold him into slavery guiltless then? After all, they were integral to God's plan.

The idea of concurrence that we discussed earlier is essential to our understanding of our lives as well as of Joseph's. Concurrence refers to the fact that at the same time we are acting, God is acting in and through us. Everything is flowing together.

God, indeed, does ordain whatever comes to pass. The word *whatever* is inclusive. But you might remember from our earlier discussion that the *Westminster Confession* was quick to state that God is not the author of sin, nor is violence offered to the will of the creatures. God does not coerce sin, but He does permit it and uses it to bring about His purpose.

Again, second causes are not nullified. God sent Joseph to Egypt by a second cause, his wicked brothers' selling him into slavery. What a perfect example of a second cause—a wicked one—being an integral part of God's good plan to provide grain for Jacob's family twenty years in the future. Joseph did not mitigate the brothers' guilt:

> "You meant evil against me; but God meant it for good."
> (Genesis 50:20)

The brothers were guilty of a heinous crime, but God was working through their crime to fulfill His purpose. They meant it for evil. Their intent was evil. God meant it for good. God's intent is always good. How bewilderingly beautiful providence is!

2. What if Joseph had not related the two dreams he had as a youth to his brothers? Would history have been altered?

> Joseph had a dream, and he told it to his brothers; and they hated him even more. . . . Then he dreamed still another dream and told it to his brothers. . . . "This time, the sun, the moon, and the eleven stars bowed down to me." . . . And his brothers envied him.
> (Genesis 37:5, 9-11)

Joseph's brothers already hated Joseph because he was Jacob's favorite son. Joseph's sharing his dreams with his already jealous and envious brothers clearly precipitated their determination to rid their family of their father's favorite.

"What if" Joseph had kept the dreams to himself? Would the brothers have envied him but not harmed him? Would Joseph have remained in his father's house and missed out on slavery, imprisonment, and twenty years of separation from his family? Yes. But there would have been no one for the brothers to buy grain from in Egypt because no one would have stored the grain up during the seven years of plenty. Only Joseph could interpret the dream God gave Pharaoh, remember?

Because God governs the details of lives, Joseph shared his dreams with his brothers. He therefore fell victim to their envy and jealousy. But behind it all was a God with the power to govern his creatures with a good intent in dispatching Joseph to Egypt for future service. Exactly what God meant to take place did take place within the idea of concurrence. Astonishing, isn't it?

Folks are often tempted to play the "what if" game. "What if" my father hadn't deserted us? Would my life have been different? Certainly. Do you ever think about your life this way? Do you think through history this way? It is an entertaining exercise. It becomes a profitable exercise only when you realize that the "what ifs" don't matter. "What ifs" assume that many sets of outcomes are possible. We know that there has always been only one outcome possible because God has always been working out His plan. It is, after all, His story.

Ultimately, thankfulness arises from the realization that God does govern the details of our lives as well as the details of Joseph's life. God is governing "all things." There are no "what ifs" in God's mind; they are only in our minds.
Please apply these thoughts to your own life.

3. Was Joseph aware that God's "invisible hand" was directing his life the day he was sold to Potiphar?

The Bible doesn't tell us, but the lad must have been bewildered by his brothers' treatment, the roughness of the Ishmaelite caravan's march, and his sale to a stranger, a foreigner. He was not yet twenty years of age.

Adam Smith, in his book *The Wealth of Nations,* termed providence "the invisible hand of God." R. C. Sproul has written a fine book with this title, which I heartily recommend to you. It is aimed at an understanding of providence that is of a far greater depth than my humble effort here.

The invisible hand of God. Once you begin to see it in a life like Joseph's, you begin to see it in history. Once you see it in history, you begin asking how the invisible hand is moving in your own life. Excitement, significance, and purpose follow. At the beginning I warned you that the study of providence would change your view of all of history as well as your view of the history of your own life. *To examine life without a view to providence is to misunderstand life.* Do you agree?

> True knowledge is rather "the consistency and agreement of our ideas with the ideas of God."
> —Author Unknown

Joseph was a man of faith, which he admirably evidenced during the lengthy separation from his family and his own culture. How he resisted the advances of Potiphar's wife is difficult to comprehend but easy to commend. Can you imagine the difficulty it posed for a young man to be pursued daily by a beautiful and powerful woman who bluntly requested, "Lie with me"? The Scriptures add,

> So it was, as she spoke to Joseph day by day, that he did not heed her, to lie with her or to be with her. . . . She caught him by the garment, saying, "Lie with me." But he left his garment in her hand, and fled and ran outside.
> (Genesis 39:10-12)

Before Joseph fled, he attempted to reason with Potiphar's wife:

> "How then can I do this great wickedness, and sin against God?"
> (Genesis 39:9)

Did Joseph have the early Scriptures with him? Not in scroll form, but they were undoubtedly written on his heart and mind. How did he maintain his integrity without anyone else to worship with in this pagan country? That must be attributed to God-given grace and faith.

Joseph may or may not have been aware of God's "invisible hand" guiding his life the day he was sold to Potiphar, but it's clear he was aware that God was watching the day he was tempted by Potiphar's wife.

Are you cognizant of God's ever-watchful eye in your daily walk? It's there, you know. He's ever-present. Are you now thoughtful about God's "invisible hand" in your life? I hope so. Contemplation of His ever-watchful eyes and ever-moving hand has affected my life in a manner that's difficult for me to quantify but easy for me to be thankful for. May the same prove true for you.

4. Joseph rose to an elevated position in Potiphar's household. Later, he also rose in responsibility while he was in prison. Finally, he became the second most important man in Egypt. What part of these advancements should be attributed to God, and what part should be attributed to Joseph?

I pose this question in order to raise and refute an objection that often arises during a discussion of God's providence. Thoughtful people worry that we are all just "puppets." But the notion of human marionettes whose every action is mechanically controlled by God is repugnant to the biblical concept of providence.

Joseph freely reported the wrong his brothers did to his father, and as well, freely shared his dreams with his brothers. Joseph freely worked diligently in Potiphar's household, and his wisdom and diligence were duly noted. His elevation followed. His hard work, brilliance, and wisdom were evident, even in a foreign culture. He was promoted and rewarded for his good qualities.

God, of course, as I am laboring to prove, governed Joseph's placement in Egypt in general, and in Potiphar's home in particular. Joseph's temptation by way of Potiphar's wife was governed so that Joseph would land in prison and meet the butler God would later utilize to commend Joseph to Pharaoh.

Are we all agreed so far? Joseph was diligent while God governed his diligence. Yet there is an underlying principle I wish to reach in order to exalt God's grace. Who made Joseph handsome? Who made Joseph diligent? Who made Joseph wise? Who placed Joseph in a family that had the patriarch Jacob as its head? Plainly, God is to be praised for "all things" pertaining to Joseph and his life.

What about your life? Who made you as you are? Who made you what you are? Who made you successful or beautiful or bright? Who chose your family?

Allow me to paraphrase C. S. Lewis: Modesty rises and leaves the room when humility enters. It's still true isn't it? Let's revisit a passage we hurried by previously:

> Now these things, brethren, I have figuratively transferred to myself and Apollos for your sakes, that you may learn in us not to think beyond what is written, that none of you may be puffed up on behalf of one against the other. For who makes you differ from another? And what do you have that you did not receive? Now if you did indeed receive it, why do you boast as if you had not received it?
> (1 Corinthians 4:6-7)

Paul is discoursing against pride and self-conceit, which had fractured the church at Corinth, but the light he shines will smite our own lives equally well.

The ministers at the head of the factions in the church at Corinth encouraged rather than discouraged the ongoing feud. Paul asked what they were boasting in. After all, hadn't their particular gifts come from God's hand? They had *received* their gifts, right? To take to themselves the glory for their gifts would be to steal the glory from its rightful recipient, God.

The gifts they had were debts to God, not things to boast of and glory in. Debts call forth duties.

What of us? What of your gifts? Do you boast about your attainments? Aren't they all owing to God's grace and gifts? Boasting is not an option. All that you are and have achieved is owing to grace. If you have received all that you have, what could you call your own? If you have *received* all that you have, what could you possibly be prideful about? Great gifts honor God when those in possession of them are humble and praise God for them rather than take the praise for themselves:

> Not unto us, O Lord, not unto us,
> But to Your name give glory.
> (Psalm 115:1)

If we weighed our gifts correctly, arrogance and self-conceit would evaporate. Joseph did his part, and God governed all. Underlying this statement is our knowledge that all the character and characteristics Joseph had were authored and governed by God, too.

5. Pharaoh had a dream. How does God cause an unbeliever like Pharaoh to dream anything?

The "how" is beyond my understanding; however, the Scripture plainly teaches,

> The dreams of Pharaoh are one; God has shown
> Pharaoh what He is about to do.
> (Genesis 41:25)

God, by special providence, filled Pharaoh's head with a vexing dream. The two prisoners Joseph had met in prison had virtually the same testimony. God had filled their heads with unusual dreams that made extraordinary impressions on them.

> God has immediate access to the spirits of men, which He can make serviceable to His own purposes whenever He pleases, quite beyond the

intention of those concerned. To Him all hearts are open.
—Matthew Henry

Our God is in Heaven;
He does whatever He pleases.
(Psalm 115:3)

"All things" are done according to the counsel of His will. He exerts a universal, uncontrollable influence whenever and wherever He pleases. God is sovereign.

6. Jacob bewails his fate in Genesis 42:36: "You have bereaved me: Joseph is no more, Simeon is no more, and you want to take Benjamin. All these things are against me." Was Jacob wrong?

Jacob's sons had just reported the distress they had encountered in Egypt while attempting to purchase grain. To ensure their return, it was necessary that they leave Simeon behind as surety. If they brought their youngest brother, Benjamin, on their return trip, all would be well. Who could have imagined all that had befallen them since they first departed?

Jacob is frightened and disheartened. In kindness, Joseph had returned Jacob's money, and Jacob, knowing the character of his sons, feared that something was amiss. Why did the boys still have their money? Did they obtain the grain fraudulently?

Jacob concluded that "all things" were against him. Joseph was dead, Simeon imprisoned, and Benjamin soon to be gone. At the very moment that Jacob reckoned that "all things" were against him, God was providentially working "all things" together for good. Joseph was alive and prominent; Simeon had never been safer, and Benjamin was deeply beloved by this Egyptian overlord. *Jacob was blind to the true facts; God was not.* Jacob's view of his life and the world could hardly have been more inaccurate.

My life has been much the same. I have, for want of faith, perplexed myself about matters that God was well aware of. I've fussed about news I've received, misreading it. Like Jacob, I've felt that "all things" were against me at times. Like Jacob, I was wrong. Most of what I've feared was against me has proved to be for me. God has caused "all things" to work together for my good, just as He promised.

What of you? Is your bodily health failing? Is slander filling your friends' ears? Are there accusations on the lips of your worst enemies, as well as of your closest relatives? Does your fortune now belong to someone else? If you are a believer, the truth is that all these things you think are working against you are really working for you an eternal weight of glory.

Let me ask you one more time: Do you believe that "all things" are against you? If you do, you're dead wrong. If you're a believer, "all things" are working for your good. We have God's word on it.

Jacob's misapprehensions would all shortly be corrected. May it be the same for you and me. What power, coupled with tenderness, God exhibits in Jacob's life and in ours.

To examine life without a view to providence is to misunderstand life.

Conclusion

I have endeavored, under three headings, to press upon you the truth that the Almighty actively governs us and our world: First, for believers, He makes "all things," both good and bad, to work together for good. For unbelievers, I have no such good news. God, indeed, does govern their lives, but He does not make all things work together for their good.

Second, chastening for good belongs only to believers. God has promised it, and if they are without it, they are either unaware of the chastening that is taking place or they are pretenders to faith rather than believers. God governs the chastenings of His children prudently and makes them beneficial and medicinal to His sons and daughters.

Finally, God's sovereignty and providence destroy any ignorant speculation about "chance," "accidents," "fate," and "randomness."

I'm a self-described "itinerant Bible teacher." That simply means that I will travel most anywhere to speak or to attend or conduct a Bible study. I have no formal Bible training. I have no degree. I once enrolled in a seminary but managed to be placed on probation before the first day of classes for questioning a professor's teaching on Jonah, which was included in the seminary's introductory packet. Can you imagine? Nevertheless, I believe that God has called me to teach. To say I have no formal Bible training is not to say I have no training. My instructors have mainly been the Holy Spirit and our Puritan forefathers.

Nevertheless, whenever you read an author who admits he's uneducated and untrained, it's always wise to emulate the Berean Christians of Acts 17:

> These were more fair-minded . . . and searched the Scriptures daily to find out whether these things were so.
> (Acts 17:11)

You should be doubly careful about accepting any teaching from a confessed criminal who couldn't make it to the first day of seminary classes. Please scrutinize all I've written. Search the Scriptures to see whether these things are as I say they are. I trust you'll discover that a formal education isn't required to find truth in the Scriptures. The original disciples were fishermen, laymen, weren't they?

To glorify God and to exalt His name are always my goals. Bartenders, concrete workers, Starbucks girls, and Sunday school teachers are my field. I aim for plainness, and I hope I have achieved it. Please judge my efforts charitably.

If my effort is helpful to you in any way, thank the Master for it.

Please apply the lessons you've learned about God's providence to your life and your understanding of the world. Look for evidence of God's providence in your own life. Esther, Jephthah, and Jacob did not see all the purposes of providence as they played out in their lives, but they did see some of them. May that be true for you and for me. It will be enough until we reach heaven, our true home.

If you're a believer, perhaps you're asking yourself a question that's outside the scope of this little book but one that is prompted by your new view of providence. That question is this: "How is it that I became a Christian and my sister did not? Did God sovereignly govern my interest in salvation?"

Simply stated, yes. Your salvation, *especially* your salvation, is the product of God's sovereignty. If you wish to delve into this more, you may wish to pick up another of my humble efforts, titled *A Strange Thing Happened on My Way to Hell*. It is meant to be an introduction to the truth that God is sovereign over salvation, too. It may whet your appetite to read a really good book on the subject by R. C. Sproul, *Chosen by God*.

In closing, I would put you in remembrance of something I said earlier. An understanding of providence is the key that will unlock the meaning to your life. Attempting to understand your life, the world, and history without your spectacles of providence on will only prove to be a fool's errand. *To misunderstand providence is to misunderstand every aspect of this world and the next*. I know—I was in complete darkness about it for more than forty years.

Thanks,

Bill

Cell: 217-652-3525

www.Ezraministries.com

Email: wmdmoore@hotmail.com

I told him that I was a Pilgrim, going to the Celestial City.
—John Bunyan's *Pilgrim's Progress*

Tell the folks of Tilbury Town that God converted Huck Finn.

This little effort of mine would have stalled just before the finish line if it weren't for my friend, Tracy Buck. Extraordinary people often fail to see themselves correctly. Tracy falls into this camp. She possesses the very skills I need and lack. I'm very appreciative of her help.

Thanks for reading my little book. I hope it's been a help to you.

I'm sometimes asked about the nuts and bolts of Ezra Ministries, Inc. It's quite simple, really. There is a board of directors, and I am one of them. The ministry files all reports required by the government for a 501(c)3, not-for-profit corporation. Our goal is to glorify God and exalt His Name in every way possible. Christian education is our focus.

I write books and teach whenever and wherever I'm invited. If you have a church, a para-church organization, or a book club, I'll come if you invite me.

Our materials as well as teaching videos from "Plain Talk About Life and the Bible" are available at www.ezraministries.com. I give the books I write to the ministry, and I receive no royalties from them.

All of our books and music CDs are made available at no charge. We do accept gifts should you choose to give one. If you cannot afford to support the ministry, please don't. If you can afford to give, please consider doing so. As I mentioned earlier, we are a 501(c)3 corporation, which makes your gift tax-deductible.

In Christ's love,

Bill

Ezra Ministries, Inc., Loami, Illinois
Mailing Address:
P.O. Box 428
Winnetka, IL 60093
217-652-3525

Most men are content to live
without knowing why
—W. D. Moore

HIS STORY

We believed him forsaken of heaven,
And likewise disinherited by hell;
Neither saint nor devil - not fit to dwell
With God's angels nor with Satan's minions.
We drove life's intruder out of Eden,
Toward the gates of hades, knowing well
God would smile. Tob was his oven and cell,
The earth's worthless rabble his brethren.

Conquerors are steeped in adversity
By the unseen; history's Smitty fans
His fires and the hammer and anvil free
The prisoner from our designs and plans
His hero polished. Why couldn't I see
History is the Deity's, not man's?

-- W.D. Moore